# Regional Equity

Regional equity as a field of scholarship, as an arena of policy change, and as a social movement has grown, diversified, and matured in important ways over the past decade. The fruits of that growth and development can be seen in recent federal and state policies, in the practices of many regional planning organizations, and in the agendas and approaches of countless community-based organizations and issue advocacy groups.

As the field has expanded, a growing number of researchers have been tracking these phenomena: explaining how and why concepts of metropolitan development are being reframed; documenting the efforts to shape policies and diversify leadership; and assessing where and how equity and social justice concerns have been brought into regional planning for transportation, land use, housing, public finances, environmental quality, smart growth, sustainable development, public health, and other issue areas. This volume brings together analyses and commentary by some of the leading scholarly observers these timely developments.

This book was published as a special issue of *Community Development*.

**Victor Rubin** is a Vice President for Research at PolicyLink, a research and action institute advancing social and economic equity based in Oakland, CA, USA. He served as Director of the HUD Office of University Partnerships. He was formerly Adjunct Associate Professor of City and Regional Planning at University of California, Berkeley, where he earned his MCP and PhD.

# Community Development—Current Issues Series

Edited by
Paul Lachapelle, *Montana State University, USA*

The Community Development Society (CDS) in conjunction with Routledge/Taylor & Francis is pleased to present this series of volumes on current issues in community development. The series is designed to present books organized around special topics or themes, promoting exploration of timely and relevant issues impacting both community development practice and research. Building on a rich history of over 40 years of publishing the journal, *Community Development*, the series will provide reprints of special issues and collections from the journal. Each volume is updated with the editor's introductory chapter, bringing together current applications around the topical theme.

Founded in 1970, the CDS is a professional association serving both researchers and practitioners. CDS actively promotes the continued advancement of the practice and knowledge base of community development. For additional information about CDS, visit www.comm-dev.org.

You can see further details about this series on the Routledge website on http://www.routledge.com/books/series/CDS/

**Tourism, Planning, and Community Development**
*Edited by Rhonda G. Phillips*

**Community Development Approaches to Improving Public Health**
*Edited by Robert Ogilvie*

**Community Economic Development**
*Edited by Rhonda Phillips and Terry L. Besser*

**Community Leadership Development**
Theory, Research and Application
*Edited by Mark A. Brennan*

**Cooperatives and Community Development**
*Edited by Rhonda Phillips and Vanna Gonzales*

**Local Food and Community Development**
*Edited by Gary Paul Green and Rhonda Phillips*

**Developing Sustainable Agriculture and Community**
*Edited by Lionel J. Beaulieu and Jeffrey L. Jordan*

**Sustainable Rural Development**
Sustainable Livelihoods and the Community Capitals Framework
*Edited by Mary Emery, Isabel Gutierrez-Montes and Edith Fernandez-Baca*

**Innovative Community Change Practices**
*Edited by Norman Walzer and Sam Cordes*

**Community Visioning Programs**
Processes and Outcomes
*Edited by Norman Walzer and Gisele F. Hamm*

**Innovative Measurement and Evaluation of Community Development Practices**
*Edited by Norman Walzer, Jane Leonard and Mary Emery*

**Innovative Community Responses to Disaster**
*Edited by Brent D. Hales, Norman Walzer and James R. Calvin*

**Rural Wealth Creation as a Sustainable Economic Development Strategy**
*Edited by Shanna Ratner and Deborah Markley*

**Regional Equity**
*Edited by Victor Rubin*

**Food & Fitness Community Partnerships**
*Edited by Laurie Lachance, Lauri Carpenter, Mary Emery and Mia Luluquisen*

# Regional Equity

*Edited by*
**Victor Rubin**

LONDON AND NEW YORK

First published 2016
by Routledge
2 Park Square, Milton Park, Abingdon, Oxon, OX14 4RN, UK

and by Routledge
711 Third Avenue, New York, NY 10017, USA

*Routledge is an imprint of the Taylor & Francis Group, an informa business*

© 2016 Community Development Society

All rights reserved. No part of this book may be reprinted or reproduced or utilised in any form or by any electronic, mechanical, or other means, now known or hereafter invented, including photocopying and recording, or in any information storage or retrieval system, without permission in writing from the publishers.

*Trademark notice*: Product or corporate names may be trademarks or registered trademarks, and are used only for identification and explanation without intent to infringe.

*British Library Cataloguing in Publication Data*
A catalogue record for this book is available from the British Library

ISBN 13: 978-1-138-18355-1

Typeset in TimesNewRomanPS
by diacriTech, Chennai

**Publisher's Note**
The publisher accepts responsibility for any inconsistencies that may have arisen during the conversion of this book from journal articles to book chapters, namely the possible inclusion of journal terminology.

**Disclaimer**
Every effort has been made to contact copyright holders for their permission to reprint material in this book. The publishers would be grateful to hear from any copyright holder who is not here acknowledged and will undertake to rectify any errors or omissions in future editions of this book.

# Contents

|  |  |  |
|---|---|---|
|  | *Citation Information* | ix |
|  | *Notes on Contributors* | xi |
| 1. | Guest Editor's introduction: regional equity<br>Victor Rubin | 1 |
| 2. | For what it's worth: regional equity, community organizing, and metropolitan America<br>Manuel Pastor, Chris Benner and Martha Matsuoka | 4 |
| 3. | Spatial justice through regionalism? The inside game, the outside game, and the quest for the spatial fix in the United States<br>Karen Chapple and Edward G. Goetz | 25 |
| 4. | The role of community-based strategies in addressing metropolitan segregation and racial health disparities<br>Malo André Hutson and Sacoby Wilson | 43 |
| 5. | Smart growth principles and the management of urban sprawl<br>Robert Blair and Gerard Wellman | 61 |
| 6. | Regional equity through community development planning: the Metro Detroit Regional Investment Initiative<br>Jane Morgan and Sujata Shetty | 78 |
| 7. | A model to embed health outcomes into land-use planning<br>Pam Moore | 92 |
|  | *Index* | 109 |

# Citation Information

The chapters in this book were originally published in *Community Development*, volume 42, issue 4 (October 2011). When citing this material, please use the original page numbering for each article, as follows:

**Chapter 1**
*Guest Editor's introduction: regional equity*
Victor Rubin
*Community Development*, volume 42, issue 4 (October 2011) pp. 434–436

**Chapter 2**
*For what it's worth: regional equity, community organizing, and metropolitan America*
Manuel Pastor, Chris Benner and Martha Matsuoka
*Community Development*, volume 42, issue 4 (October 2011) pp. 437–457

**Chapter 3**
*Spatial justice through regionalism? The inside game, the outside game, and the quest for the spatial fix in the United States*
Karen Chapple and Edward G. Goetz
*Community Development*, volume 42, issue 4 (October 2011) pp. 458–475

**Chapter 4**
*The role of community-based strategies in addressing metropolitan segregation and racial health disparities*
Malo André Hutson and Sacoby Wilson
*Community Development*, volume 42, issue 4 (October 2011) pp. 476–493

**Chapter 5**
*Smart growth principles and the management of urban sprawl*
Robert Blair and Gerard Wellman
*Community Development*, volume 42, issue 4 (October 2011) pp. 494–510

**Chapter 6**
*Regional equity through community development planning: the Metro Detroit Regional Investment Initiative*
Jane Morgan and Sujata Shetty
*Community Development*, volume 42, issue 4 (October 2011) pp. 511–524

CITATION INFORMATION

**Chapter 7**
*A model to embed health outcomes into land-use planning*
Pam Moore
*Community Development*, volume 42, issue 4 (October 2011) pp. 525–540

For any permission-related enquiries please visit:
http://www.tandfonline.com/page/help/permissions

# Notes on Contributors

**Chris Benner** is a Professor of Environmental Studies and Sociology at the University of California, Santa Cruz, CA, USA. He is also the Director of the Everett Program on Digital Tools for Social Innovation. His research focuses on regional labor markets and changes in work patterns. His recent publications include *Just Growth: Inclusion and Prosperity in America's Metropolitan Region* (Routledge, 2012), co-authored by Manual Pastor.

**Robert Blair** is a Professor of Urban Studies at the University of Nebraska Omaha, Omaha, NE, USA. His research interests include policy implementation, economic and community development, and public management. He has published in a number of journals, including the *International Journal of Economic Development* and *Community Development: Journal of the Community Development Society*.

**Karen Chapple** is a Professor of City and Regional Planning at the University of California, Berkeley, CA, USA. She specializes in community and economic development, housing, and regional planning, and recently published *Planning Sustainable Cities and Regions: Towards More Equitable Development* (Routledge, 2014).

**Edward G. Goetz** is a Professor of Urban and Regional Planning and Director of the Center for Urban and Regional Affairs at the University of Minnesota, Minneapolis, MN, USA. His research focuses on issues of race and poverty in housing policy implementation and planning. His most recent book is *New Deal Ruins: Race, Economic Justice, and Public Housing Policy* (2013).

**Malo André Hutson** is an Assistant Professor in the Department of City and Regional Planning at the University of California, Berkeley, CA, USA. He is author of the forthcoming book, *The Urban Struggle for Economic, Environmental, and Social Justice: Deepening Their Roots*, which will form part of Routledge's *Equity, Justice, and the Sustainable City* series.

**Martha Matsuoka** is an Associate Professor of Urban and Environmental Policy at the University of California, Los Angeles, CA, USA. Her research interests include sustainable community development, social movements, metropolitan regionalism, and environmental justice. She is co-author of *This Could Be the Start of Something Big: Regional Equity and America's Metropolitan Future* (2009).

**Pam Moore** is an Environmental Health Officer at the Interior Health Authority, British Columbia, Canada. She works with local governments to include healthy public policy within their land-use practices, and with the overall goal of improving public health.

# NOTES ON CONTRIBUTORS

**Jane Morgan** is President of JFM Consulting Group, Detroit, MI, USA. Her work involves engaging organizations and institutions in developing strategies and evaluating programs and initiatives that address the challenges facing urban and historically underrepresented communities. She works with a range of organizations in the nonprofit, philanthropic and public sectors, with a focus on community and economic development and health.

**Manuel Pastor** is a Professor of Sociology and American Studies and Ethnicity at the University of Southern California, Los Angeles, CA, USA. His current research focuses on low-income communities and the social, environmental, and economic challenges that face them. His latest book, co-authored by Chris Benner, is *Equity, Growth and Community: What the Nation Can Learn from America's Metro Areas* (2015).

**Victor Rubin** is a Vice President for Research at PolicyLink, a research and action institute advancing social and economic equity based in Oakland, CA, USA. He served as Director of the HUD Office of University Partnerships. He was formerly Adjunct Associate Professor of City and Regional Planning at University of California, Berkeley, where he earned his MCP and PhD.

**Sujata Shetty** is an Associate Professor in the Department of Geography and Planning at the University of Toledo, Toledo, OH, USA. She specializes in community and economic development planning, gender and planning, and international development. Her recent publications include "Dealing with Decline in Old Industrial Cities in Europe and the United States: Problems and Policies" in *Built Environment*, and "Global Challenges and Local Responses: Creating a New Urban World in the Shrinking Cities of the U.S. Industrial Midwest", in *Regional Science Policy and Practice*.

**Gerard Wellman** is an Assistant Professor at the Department of Politics and Public Administration, California State University, Stanislaus, CA, USA. His research interests include community development, active and public transportation, social justice theory, and urban affairs. He has published in a number of journals, including *Public Administration Quarterly*, *Journal of Community Development*, and *Public Works Management & Policy*.

**Sacoby Wilson** is an Assistant Professor at the Maryland Institute for Applied Environmental Health, School of Public Health, University of Maryland, College Park, MD, USA where he directs the Initiative on Community Engagement, Environmental Justice, and Health (CEEJH). Dr. Wilson works in partnership with community-based organizations to understand and address environmental injustice and health disparities. Dr. Wilson has published in *Environmental Research*, *Environmental Justice*, the *American Journal of Public Health (AJPH)*, *Environmental Health*, and the *International Journal of Environmental Research and Public Health (IJERPH)*.

# Guest Editor's introduction: regional equity

Regional equity as a field of scholarship, as an arena of policy change, and as a social movement, has grown, diversified, and matured in important ways over the past decade. The fruits of that growth and development can be seen in new federal and state policies, in the practices of many regional planning organizations, and in the agendas and approaches of countless community-based organizations and issue advocacy groups. As the field has expanded, a growing number of researchers have been tracking these phenomena: explaining how and why concepts of metropolitan development are being reframed, documenting the efforts to shape policies and diversify leadership; assessing where and how equity and social justice concerns have been brought into regional planning for transportation, land use, housing, public finances, environmental quality, smart growth, sustainable development, public health, and other issue areas. They have also been creating metrics for measuring the outcomes and impacts of the new regional plans and policies.

This special issue of the *Journal* brings together analyses and commentary by some of the leading scholarly observers of these timely developments. Its origins lie in discussions between former *Journal* editor Ted Bradshaw and me several years ago, as we reflected back upon the mix of researchers, policy-makers, community developers, and advocates who convened every three years at the PolicyLink Regional Equity Summits, beginning in 2002.[1] Many of the participants were community developers, community organizers, or community builders, previously working only at the neighborhood level, and their new attachment to a regional scale and perspective was an important evolution in their thinking and actions. Each Summit has been a touchstone for the growth of regional equity as a movement, a venue in which to learn about new policies and programs, and, fortuitously, a setting for the engagement of scores of faculty and graduate students in community development, city and regional planning, public health, economics, sociology, and many other disciplines and professions. We thought it would be valuable to pull together new research that reflected this diversity and these kinds of contributions. The range of potential materials was continually growing, as regional equity topics became more frequent in academic conferences and at the leading policy gatherings in smart growth, sustainable development, environmental policy, transportation, housing, and other fields of practice.

A definition of regional equity from an activist perspective, introduced at the 2008 Summit, reads as follows:

In the broadest sense, regional equity is a framework for social change that is nestled within, and inseparable from, the quest for economic and social justice in America. Regional equity brings a unique perspective to the broader equity movement: a deep understanding of how metropolitan development patterns structure the life chances and social and economic opportunities of residents, and the ways in which uneven spatial development reinforces old racial and class divides, while creating new ones. The goal is to ensure that everyone – regardless of the neighborhood in which they live – has access to essential ingredients for economic and social success: living-wage jobs, viable housing choices, public transportation, good schools, strong social networks, safe, and walkable streets, services, parks, access to healthy food, and so on. As a framework for action, regional equity offers an *analysis* of the root causes and dynamics that create and perpetuate inequity and a *toolkit* of strategies, principles, and methods for advancing equity and opportunity in regions.[2]

We are fortunate to include in this collection articles whose range, when taken as a whole, exemplify the diversity of issues, disciplines and stances addressed in that definition. There are, broadly speaking, three kinds of scholarship that are relevant to the regional equity framework. First there is the examination of this phenomenon as a social movement, a new focus for policy and for organizing. Such studies, whether of a single metropolitan area or of the national movement, are sometimes done by scholars who are also contributors to the efforts they are documenting, but they are analyzing these developments with critical distance and valuable comparative perspective. The article by Pastor, Benner, and Matsuoka describes, and analyzes these trends on a national scale, a subject amplified in their 2009 book, *This Could be the Start of Something Big: How Social Movements for Regional Equity are Reshaping Metropolitan America*. They explain how strands of innovation in regionalism, community development, and organizing converged in the actions of a host of groups based in faith-based social justice, labor rights, environmental justice, housing access, and other arenas. Chapple and Goetz describe "equity regionalism" and raise questions about the viability of achieving expanded opportunity and social justice through policies to promote the spatial deconcentration of poverty on a metropolitan scale.

Second, there are new types of regional analysis: new ways of explaining metropolitan-level trends in population, housing, transportation, economic change, public health and other subjects. This kind of research assesses the state of equity and, sometimes, points toward possible policy strategies to address disparities and promote equitable development. The article by Hutson and Wilson, which focuses on a regional analysis of health outcomes in the context of patterns of racial segregation, is an example of this kind of research.

Third, and one that is only recently emerging, are studies of the recent policy changes and innovative forms of regional planning and decision-making. As the scores of new federal regional Sustainable Communities partnerships are implemented beginning in 2011, there will be plenty of new material for not only program evaluation but also broader applied research about the role of regional equity in that initiative. The article by Blair in this collection, on measuring sprawl and growth management, represents one of the earlier efforts to create new methods by which to systematically assess outcomes relevant to regional equity, and foreshadows some of the techniques we see being applied in the new initiatives. Morgan and Shetty examine how regional equity objectives fared in one metropolitan area – Detroit – where community developers gave explicit programmatic attention to areas at the boundaries of the central city and its first ring of suburbs. Moore's article further illustrates the importance of partnerships, at a variety of levels, via the story of British Columbia's model programs to connect public health with land use planning.

I also want to acknowledge the foundational scholarship on regional equity which has helped to document the movement and define the themes developed in the field and in this journal issue. *Breakthrough Communities: Sustainability and Justice in the Next American Metropolis*, the 2009 volume edited by Paloma Pavel, features the voices of many of the local leaders of the regional equity movement, collected through years of collaboration with those leaders. *Growing Smarter: Achieving Livable Communities, Environmental Justice, and Regional Equity*, edited by Robert D. Bullard in 2007, was one of the first volumes to express and codify the critique of smart growth from the perspective of low income communities of color. Both books have forwards by Carl Anthony, who has done as much as anyone to advance regional equity in all its forms.

The response to the call for papers on this topic was substantial, and for reasons of timing and space, several articles which were originally submitted for this special issue were already published, or will soon appear, in future editions of the *Journal*. This is another indicator of the integration of regional equity topics into the mainstream of community development research, and we certainly hope that this trend will continue.

Editor Rhonda Phillips and the staff of the *Journal* have been steadfast in seeing this special issue through a number of unexpected changes and challenges, and I thank them and all the contributors and reviewers for their creativity, patience, and diligence.

**Notes**
1. The first Summit was held in Los Angeles in 2002, the second in Philadelphia in 2005, the third in New Orleans in 2008, and the fourth in Detroit in 2011.
2. *Regional Equity and the Quest for Full Inclusion*. Angela Glover Blackwell and Sarah Treuhaft, PolicyLink, 2008.

Victor Rubin
*Vice President for Research, PolicyLink, Oakland, CA, USA*

# For what it's worth: regional equity, community organizing, and metropolitan America

Manuel Pastor[a], Chris Benner[b] and Martha Matsuoka[c]

[a]*University of Southern California, Program for Environmental & Regional Equity, USA;* [b]*University of California, Davis, California, USA;* [c]*Occidental College, Los Angeles, California, USA*

> Regional equity has taken off as a field of research and activism in recent years. Within the general field, three important variants have emerged: community development regionalism, in which the main interest is in using regional levers to promote a new form of community revitalization; policy change regionalism, in which the main emphasis is on shifting government rules to better distribute metropolitan resources; and social movement regionalism, in which the focus is on mobilizing communities for collective action at a regional level. Drawing on a series of case studies from across the country, we argue that all these variants have a role but that social movement regionalism may be particularly effective in productively addressing the inevitable tensions and conflicts that emerge in regional equity strategies, including the relationship to business-oriented regionalism, labor–community alliances, and the role of race. We conclude by speculating on the recent efforts of social movement regionalism to scale up, suggesting that this could present an important contribution to a broader and deeper movement for progressive social change in the United States.

## Introduction

In November 2002, PolicyLink – a national intermediary focused on issues of community development and community building – worked with a group of funders and other organizations to develop and host a "National Summit" on "Promoting Regional Equity." Held in Los Angeles, a place traditionally viewed as an anathema to regional collaboration or coordination, the organizers quietly prayed that at least 300 people would gather to discuss the ideas around regional organizing and policy that had been bubbling up around the country. The low expectations were reasonable: many of the people and organizations PolicyLink sought to include in the big tent of "regional equity" thought of themselves as community developers, labor union leaders, smart growth advocates, community organizers, urban planners, faith-based activists, and/or environmental justice proponents – almost anything but equity-oriented regionalists.

What happens if you throw a party and nobody comes? Fortunately, PolicyLink did not have to find out: over 600 individuals showed, swamping the facility that had been designated for the conference. Enthusiastic and spirited conversations marked the event – but also struggle, as participants tried to come to grips with whether they really did intersect and how. Most striking was the honest admission by many attendees that tackling the large regional forces that had created the contemporary metropolitan mess was going to require a whole series of new partnerships and capacities.

Fast forward two and a half years to May 2005: "The Second National Summit," this time in Philadelphia and this time labeled "Advancing Regional Equity." Over 1300 people showed up, roughly twice the goal set by the event organizers. While there were some notable gaps in geographic representation, especially the South and the Mountain West, participants hailed from all around the country. Once again, debate was vigorous: in one particularly heated session, residents from nearby Camden, New Jersey, decried "regional equity" as an outside imposition that was producing gentrification and shifting resources away from the city to inner ring suburbs, all in the name of making a regional connection.

Fast forward once again nearly three years to March 2008, when "Regional Equity 08: The Third National Summit on Equitable Development, Social Justice and Smart Growth" was held in New Orleans. This time, nearly 2000 participants gathered for an in-depth assessment of strategies and policies to better connect low-income communities to resources and opportunities. In the background lay the wreckage of Katrina, and the scars of poverty it had revealed, and in the air was talk of building a new regional equity movement that could combat the slow-motion unnatural disasters occurring in so many cities, suburbs, and rural areas. Debate was vigorous once again: where was this movement really headed? What was its relationship to national politics? How could it begin to fully incorporate the opportunities opened by climate change initiatives and the promise of green jobs?

Big crowds and vibrant conversations – in the well-known opening words of a protest song of the 1960s, "there's something happening here ... " The regional equity perspective has clearly gained traction, supported by growing research on the importance of regions to the evolution of economic, environmental and social inequalities, and prompted by the organizing strategies of numerous community-based, labor, and even business-oriented organizations. So something is happening but, as noted in the equally famous second line of that protest song, "What it is ain't exactly clear."

Part of the problem is that perspectives take some time to gain a fixed form. While this is characteristic of any paradigm, there is also a problem peculiar to regional equity thinking. Because many of the early proponents of regional equity have tended to stress collaboration and commonality, including the compatibility of economic growth, environmental protection, and a fairer distribution of resources (see, for example, Pastor, Dreier, Grigsby, & Garza, 2000), they have been able to develop unlikely alliances, such as those between inner-city activists and suburban green-space advocates. But while an "optimal level of fog" might be useful in an early period, being analytically clear about the strands that comprise the regional equity perspective may be helpful as organizations navigate the tensions, tightropes and inevitable conflicts that arise on the ground.

In this article, we draw on a multi-year engagement with, and research on, innovative regional equity strategies from around the country (Pastor, Benner, & Matsuoka, 2009). We argue that the regional equity perspective can be understood to consist of three main variants: *community development regionalism*, in which the main interest is using regional levers to promote a new form of community revitalization; *policy reform regionalism*, in which the primary emphasis is on shifting government rules to better distribute metropolitan resources; and (3) *social movement regionalism*, in which the principal goal is to build on a sense of grievance in order to mobilize communities for mass collective action at a regional level.

These three variants share much in common, but also have significantly different constituencies, unequal access to resources, and sometimes differing strategies. Furthermore, all three types of regional equity advocates are not operating in a vacuum. They have to interact with a range of other regional initiatives, including business-sponsored public-private collaborations and a more planning-oriented and environmentally-oriented emphasis on smart growth; some of these other frameworks will have equity as a secondary goal at best, and an afterthought at worst. Finally, at least one of these variants – social movement regionalism – is bound to cause conflict: indeed, it is intended to do exactly that.

We do think there is a way to thread together the three variants under one regional equity tent: the community developers work on projects that demonstrate what is possible, the policy reform strategists focus on changing policy to make the possible the norm, and the social movement regionalist build power to shift politics and thus policy. We privilege, however, the social movement element, recognizing that the nitty-gritty of constituency mobilization and regional coalition-building is not merely a method to change tax rules and zoning regulations; we see it (as so do the activists pursuing it) as a way to lay the groundwork, region by region, community by community, for the revitalization of a national progressive movement.

We begin below by elaborating on the three main types of regional equity. Drawing from cases in our longer study (Pastor, Benner, & Matsuoka, 2009), we then turn to an examination of how regional equity advocates are addressing some of the tensions and tightropes of power-building at a regional scale, including tensions between different types of regional equity initiatives, tensions with other regional initiatives – particularly those rooted in business-led initiatives – and tensions related to racial dynamics within regional equity initiatives. Our concluding section discusses ways in which regional equity activists are trying to scale up to state and national levels to impact and shore up progressive politics in America.

**Understanding regional equity**

There are many ways to slice and dice the emerging regional equity framework. One could look at philosophical or ideological views, drawing distinctions between those rooted in more or less radical approaches to analysis or organizing. One could examine issue areas, clumping together those who take on transportation, those who tackle housing, and those who focus on environmental disparities. One could perform a breakdown of constituent bases, analyzing whether the main supporters for any particular variant of the regional equity perspective stem from labor, community groups, community developers, urban officials, or struggling suburban mayors.

Here, we take a different tack, one related to an analytical frame that we find more compelling: the distinction between projects, policies, and politics. We suggest that community development regionalism has as its focus the use of regional tools to achieve particular *projects* – in this view, regionalism offers a set of new strategies to achieve the traditional objectives associated with community development corporations (CDCs) and related local efforts. We postulate that policy reform regionalism focuses on changes in *policy* that affect regional distribution of resources – this perspective is often not associated with any particular constituency, and it tends to be more focused on technical issues and collaboration with, and persuasion of, existing policy-makers. Finally, we argue that social movement regionalism is being built by a set of advocates who have seen regionalism as a vehicle for doing *politics* – that is, for building power in the interests of building a broader coalition for social and economic justice.

## *Community development regionalism*

Community developers are among urban America's unsung heroes. They build housing where private developers have failed. They create job-training programs where both skills and opportunities are in short supply. They offer family-support programs where families are often non-traditional and under considerable economic, social, and environmental stress. Where and when they succeed, it seems like a testimony to their will and faith, a miracle of achievement against the toughest odds.

But the dramatic success stories are often cast against a backdrop of policies and practices that drain resources from the communities in which they are based. In *Inside Game, Outside Game*, David Rusk (1999) analyzes the impact of 34 "exemplary" CDCs over the 1970s and 1980s. He found that, on average, poverty rates actually rose faster in the neighborhoods in which these CDCs were operating than they did in the metropolitan areas in which they existed. There were, of course, some successes – and one can also argue that the neighborhoods might have fared worse in the absence of CDC activity. Still, Rusk (1999) suggests that CDCs might usefully shift to the "outside game" – organizing to change rules in regions so as to share tax resources and constrain outward sprawl, and working to deconcentrate the poor by promoting affordable housing in existing suburbs.

Some have argued that Rusk's (1999) frame disparages local capabilities, with critics like Imbroscio (2006) suggesting that the CDCs' failure to move the needle on poverty is mostly due to a shift to market-oriented development and a consequent de-politicization of the community development movement (Imbroscio, 2006). Others have argued that Rusk (1999) is essentially recommending a dispersal strategy – by encouraging the exodus of successful residents, we are sort of "destroying the 'hood' in order to save it." Nonetheless, reaching to the region fit well with a shift in the CDC world in the 1990s from a "bricks and mortar" approach to a focus on "community building" and comprehensive community initiatives (Walsh, 1997). This new emphasis on social fabric and "social capital" was easily extended to a notion that both challenging regional decisions and forming alliances with local and regional leaders could attract new resources and opportunities for distressed communities.

In taking this regional approach, CDCs typically aim to find a regional opportunity gone astray, use organizing to shift an adverse decision, leverage regional resources to promote better development, and generate concrete projects as a result. An excellent example is the Fruitvale Transit Village in a low-income area in Oakland: when the regional transit authority suggested building a parking lot for commuters, a local CDC helped organize residents to push the parking lot away from the station and instead create a mixed-use development that serves the community. Such leveraging of efforts – taking advantage of a regional investment to promote local development – resonate with the field's original view that "poor communities need to break the isolation that left them without powerful allies and resources in mainstream society" (Anglin & Montezemolo, 2004, p. 57). But while CDCs may find this brand of regionalism a new way to influence development, it is not clear that such organizations can be the leaders in a broader movement.

After all, CDCs have to maintain productive relations with investors, city officials, foundations, and all the other entities that help them create jobs, housing, and social services; "rocking the boat" to change regional rules can raise challenges for the basic mission of building housing and developing workforce training programs. Moreover, both the power and the accountability of CDCs are inevitably local; straying too far from that base represents a form of mission drift. Thus, in a sense, some CDCs have embraced regionalism as instrumental rather than fundamental, tactical rather than strategic. They have not discovered a whole new form of community development business; they have discovered another and perhaps more effective way to do the same business.

*Policy reform regionalism*

In trying to understand policy innovation and diffusion, political scientists have identified the concept and role of "policy entrepreneurs." The basic notion is that, in various issue fields, there exists a series of actors who may work outside the formal government structure, often in independent non-profit intermediaries. They seek to identify problems, build networks with politicians and other decision-makers interested in the problems, provide these decision-makers with appropriate research, strategies, and "frames" for understanding and solving the problem, and through this complex combination, influence policy change in a preferred direction (Mintrom, 1997; Roberts & King, 1991).

The field of regional equity has certainly seen its share of policy entrepreneurs. For example, building on ideas developed while working with Secretary Henry Cisneros at the US Department of Housing and Urban Development, Bruce Katz created the Metropolitan Policy Program at the Brookings Institution in Washington in 1996. The Program provides studies ranging from examinations of the growing foreign-born presence in America's regions to evaluations of the role of convention centers in downtown revivals to considerations of the impacts of sprawl on jobs and inner-city prospects. Its mission is framed around providing policy to support "inclusive, competitive, and sustainable" growth, often sneaking inclusivity in under the banner of restoring competitiveness.

In classic "policy entrepreneur" form, the Brookings Program goes to where key politicians may be open to its ideas and then creates an information base that can engage those policy-makers. In 2003, for example, researchers from the Program began working with newly inaugurated Pennsylvania governor (and former Philadelphia mayor) Ed Rendell to develop a set of new strategies for the state. In its December 2003 release, "Back to Prosperity: A Competitive Agenda for Renewing Pennsylvania," the Brookings team argued that sprawl was "hollowing out" Pennsylvania and weakening its attractiveness to the younger creative workers that drive economies – and that the remedy consisted of reinvestment back in older cities and suburbs, a move sure to also close the equity gap even as it restored competitiveness and fiscal health. To support the report, the release was accompanied by a series of presentations throughout the state and a spate of supportive news stories.

This was Policy Entrepreneurship 101: find an already sympathetic public official, craft research and a message that resonates with dominant concerns, and develop a set of relationships with "influentials" who can move the ideas forward. The style of policy entrepreneurship for regional equity is not limited to Brookings. The Surface Transportation Policy Project, for example, has maintained a very small staff and a very long list of coalition members, using both to shift federal transportation dollars in ways that encourage transit-oriented development. Metropolitan mapper Myron Orfield has barnstormed through the country to sell the idea of regional tax-sharing (and now school desegregation); while success in the actual tax arena has been limited, he has helped reframe the way officials see themselves in the regional tapestry. Smart Growth America has enlisted the support of local and state officials in the interest of more compact development, and the Funders' Network for Smart Growth and Livable Communities has, along with PolicyLink, helped bring major philanthropies into conversation with leaders in the regional equity arena.

What are the limits to this approach? The first problem is that at least some of these policy entrepreneurs sidestep hard issues in the interest of a mainstream "framing" that can capture the attention of current policy-makers. Using a competitiveness rationale to support central city revitalization or stressing "smart growth" rules to quietly redirect dollars to distressed neighborhoods amounts to a sort of "stealth equity" – it does not address the ongoing challenges of race and *de facto* segregation. Some therefore worry that these issues will drop off the agenda whenever the going gets tough – or if competitiveness, say, can be restored without reducing concentrated poverty (Pastor, Benner, & Rosner, 2006).

The second limitation is more fundamental. Implicit in the policy entrepreneur approach is the sense that the real task is to bring intelligent analysis to those who need it – well-framed, smart ideas (such as "smart growth" itself) can win the day. Of course, bad ideas are often persistent if they serve particular interests, and the current configuration of outward sprawl and inner-city underdevelopment does have clear winners as well as losers. While policy entrepreneurs in the regional equity field do get engaged in coalition building, they are often focused on "elite persuasion." The problem is that real change requires the development and building of broad constituencies that can keep decision-makers under pressure – policy entrepreneurs, in short, often lack the troops.

We acknowledge that our lines between policy entrepreneurship and constituency mobilization are too starkly drawn. Myron Orfield, for example, may sell his ideas to municipal decision-makers but he embraces a hard-headed politics that focuses on officials in older and less glamorous suburbs and he has found a vibrant constituency in the faith-based movements that often bring him to talk in church basements and town halls. Brookings may try to bend the ears of policy-makers but it has a cold political calculus of where its efforts will find an audience and where they will not. PolicyLink may bring funders to the table but its Regional Equity summits have also brought together community developers, public officials, and social activists alike. With all these qualifications, our analytical point is straightforward: if policy reforms are to "stick" – particularly reforms that can be controversial – mobilization, popular education, and power-building must be part of the equation.

## Social movement regionalism

Indeed, for many in the regional equity field, building power to forge a progressive movement is exactly the heartfelt point of their work. Talk to the leaders of the Los Angeles Alliance for a New Economy, acknowledged pioneers in the world of Community Benefits Agreements, and you will not linger long on the arcane details of zoning restrictions, density bonuses, and first-source hiring – instead, you find yourself quickly engaged in a conversation about what it means to reframe development, refashion coalitions, and rework the power base needed to fundamentally transform the way the economy works. Talk to the organizers of the interfaith Gamaliel Foundation, acknowledged champions of a "fix it first" approach to infrastructure, and you quickly move past the details of regional planning agencies, transit line alignment, and restrictions on low-income housing – instead, you will find yourself immersed in a conversation about the lack of connectivity in American society, and the ways in which working regionally can bring together a nation separated by geography, race and class.

That scale is important in social movement building is increasingly recognized in the academic literature. Wilton and Cranford (2002), for example, argue that "a full understanding of the political potential of social movements requires recognition of their inherently spatial nature." Jones and MacLeod (2004) distinguish between "regional spaces" and "spaces of regionalism," suggesting that the former are more economic and objective in their origin while the latter are more a created territory for political mobilization and even cultural expression. Others have argued that the region opens up new forms of organizing and regional democracy (Jonas & Pincetl, 2006), with Iris Young arguing that while the scope of polities should be regional, "[r]egional governance is deeply democratic ... only if combined with neighborhood and community-based participatory institutions" (Young, 2000, p. 9).

Putting in place these regional institutions is exactly the focus of what we call social movement regionalists. The labor-affiliated think tank, Working Partnerships in San Jose, has worked on the regional scale in terms of analysis and policy: it has issued studies on the region's key industries, highlighted the need for affordable housing in a high-tech economy, and participated in urban planning efforts aimed at livability. But its hallmark has been training a cadre of interconnected community leaders, through a series of eight-week to 12-week "Leadership Institutes" focused on labor leaders, community organizers, leaders of faith-based communities, public-sector staff and elected officials, and leaders from the small business community and ethnic business associations to develop a common understanding of the economy and analysis of power in the Silicon Valley. Working Partnerships, moreover, is working with central labor councils from Atlanta, San Diego, Miami, and New York in order to reassert labor's voice in the national debate over our nation's economic direction.

One of the most explicit versions of the social movement approach is seen in the work of SCOPE in Los Angeles. Founded by Anthony Thigpenn, a former member of the Black Panther Party and a long-time architect of precinct-based organizing and get-out-the-vote campaigns for progressive coalitions, SCOPE is a multi-dimensional social justice organization centered in South Los Angeles. For many of the organizations above, such as Gamaliel, Working Partnerships, and others, the region is important on an *objective* level: it is the scale on which inequalities are created. For SCOPE organizers, the region is perhaps more important on a *subjective* level: it is the scale at which broader patterns of inequality are actually experienced even if they are created by national policies. As such, adopting a regional perspective is an intermediate step between a more narrow consciousness of community, neighborhood and family, and a broader consciousness of society. And SCOPE, entirely self-conscious that they are movement-building, has even developed a diagram to illustrate their view and distinguish it from traditional community organizing (see Figure 1).

Weir, Rongerude, and Ansell (2007) suggest that this sort of social movement mobilization is actually key to policy change. They argue that the "horizontal collaboration" often associated with regionalism:

> ... can do little more than promote new ideas and hope for the best. Horizontal collaboration in regions may help build consensus and alliances that can work in more powerful state and federal venues to promote regional capacity ... Whether such efforts are successful depends not only on the horizontal consensus building process but, more critically, on the power relationships – alliances, coalitions, enemies – that prevail in these alternative venues. (Weir et al., 2007, p. 35)

In this view, progressive regionalism involves building multilevel power, not simply engaging in regional processes (Weir & Rongerude, 2007) – and social movement regionalists, who are explicitly focused on challenging powerful entities in the region who may gain from current development patterns, can help to build the necessary constituency power-base to ensure that alternative policies can be created and implemented.

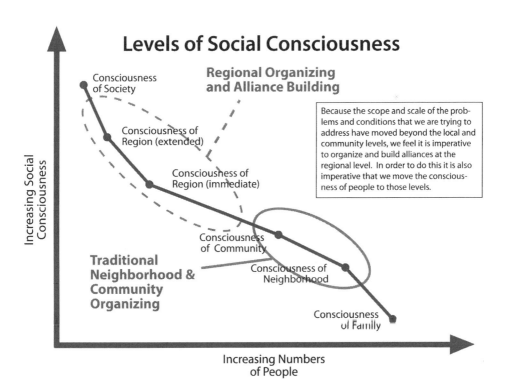

Figure 1. Levels of social consciousness by spatial scale.

While it is clear what social movements might bring to regional equity, what does regional equity bring to social movements? We think there are at least two gains. The first has to do with perspective. In his insightful study of the interfaith Gamaliel network, Kleidman (2004) argues that Gamaliel's commitment to a regional organizing approach allows its local groups to articulate a more consistent progressive vision, with a clearer analysis of processes shaping inequality and poverty, and a clearer strategy for building allies. In New Jersey, for example, Gamaliel organizers just ran – and won – a campaign to ban "regional contribution agreements," a nice phrase used to describe a vehicle for wealthy cities to avoid taking on affordable housing by giving money to poorer cities instead. The campaign was a recipe for internal conflict – struggling central cities and next-step suburbs are often at each others' throats about the leakage of poor households and attendant problems from one to the other. But organizers focused on shared fates, brought congregations together to support the effort, and even enlisted the support of home-builders and anti-sprawl environmentalists. The eventual policy victory was important, but just as critical was the way in which new and somewhat unlikely alliances were formed and sustained (Gordon, 2008).

The second contribution of regional equity to social movements is explored in more detail in the conclusion. Briefly here, for many of these organizing groups, the region is not only a new level for understanding problems and proposing solutions, it is also a new, fundamental, and strategic scale for building a broad-based social movement for justice. Such an approach to amassing national power – working one city at a time, one region at a time, one state at a time – seems to parallel the strategy once taken by the right: work from the local to the state to the national, moving hearts and minds – or as we say in the modern world, "frames" – in a way that can make a new American politics possible. Thus, regional equity is a tool in that stepping stone strategy to national transformation.

**Tensions and tightropes**

By distinguishing three types of regional equity efforts – community development regionalism, policy reform regionalism, and social movement regionalism – and associating each with one of a troika of projects, policy, and power, we are not trying to suggest that the three trends are completely separate. In the real world, groups often drift from one role to another, and all three must come together to effect change: as noted above, projects make us see the possible, policy helps make the possible standard practice, and power is what ultimately drives policy reform. All these variants of regional equity are important to the social ecology of change, although we would suggest that the social movement regionalists are critical because of their role in organizing communities to make such change actually happen.

So what is gained by making these distinctions? We think that part of the benefit has to do with some analytical clarity with regard to tensions that have bedeviled the regional equity field in general, including the relationship between communities and business, between different sorts of community organizations, and between communities themselves (particularly around issues of race). These are, of course, not the only tightropes and tensions – others include the balance of policy and politics, the mix of market and regulation, and the interplay of "inside" and "outside" games. But for those dimensions, we welcome readers to read the longer discussion in our book – you knew that was coming, right? – and more importantly, to join the debate that is raging in the field itself.

### *Bringing business in, keeping business at bay*

One of the most striking developments in recent years has been the growing business interest in regionalism. This partly reflects a well-known rescaling of economic clusters to the regional level but it also reflects business frustration with multi-jurisdictional decision-making that often stymies a competitive approach. Across the country, organizations like Joint Venture: Silicon Valley Network, Chicago Metropolis 2020, and Fund for Our Economic Future in Northeast Ohio have set a new agenda for business regionalism – and they have opened up space for equity concerns, partly from an analytical frame that recognizes the drag inequality can present for economic growth and partly from a purely political frame that seeks to expand constituency support.

Yet business is not likely to be a solid champion for social justice. Class interests have not disappeared, many businesses remain opposed to any interference with markets, and the "win–win" dreams of some regionalists are often just that – dreams. While there are numerous possibilities for securing a "double bottom line" of reasonable profits and improved community outcomes (Pastor, 2006), the real bottom line is that political struggle is required to move agendas. The problem is that community developers have to worry about their reliance on public coffers for projects while policy entrepreneurs have to keep access to elites for policy change; social movement regionalists necessarily have a more complicated and more conflictual approach.

The relationship between social movement regionalists and the business class comes in several flavors. In some cases, regional equity efforts have been driven, at least in part, by the reaction to business initiatives. The Social Equity Caucus in the Bay Area, for example, was initially created in response to regionalist tables being set by business groups like the Bay Area Council; while the Social Equity Caucus has since acquired deeper and authentic roots, partly because of its work on transportation equity and general plan revisions, it was essentially scrambling to build (and convince) its base even as it "spoke" for equity advocates. Another variant of this reaction mode can be seen in the case of Working Partnerships in San Jose.

When Joint Venture: Silicon Valley (JV:SV) was launched in 1993, the San Jose-based Santa Clara County Central Labor Council was invited to have representatives on the Board of Directors. Ultimately, John Neece from the Building Trades agreed to serve on the Board, and played an active role in JV:SV's activities. But labor council head Amy Dean, who worried that issues of equity and opportunity for disadvantaged sectors of the Valley's population would be buried under JV:SV's primary focus on economic competitiveness, decided instead to build a separate voice in the form of Working Partnerships, USA.

JV:SV actually helped build the terrain for Working Partnerships by positively reinforcing the sense of Silicon Valley as an interconnected region with a common destiny. Moreover, it served, largely unintentionally, to isolate local business opposition to labor-sponsored policy. JV:SV, after all, focused on the needs of high-technology industries and large multi-national corporations – while the San Jose Chamber of Commerce, more the province of local real estate and small business, became increasingly perceived as a creature of less forward-looking enterprises. When Working Partnerships campaigned for a Living Wage Ordinance in the City of San Jose, for example, the Chamber opposed it vehemently but JV:SV was largely silent on the issue. While JV:SV's business leaders were generally opposed to a Living Wage in principle, the policy was unlikely to affect them (as they rarely contracted directly with the City and tended to pay higher wages) and they were reluctant to offend San Jose Mayor Susan Hammer, a member of the JV:SV board and an ardent supporter of the Living Wage effort. As a result, the recalcitrant and less-connected Chamber had diminished political clout and the Living Wage passed.

JV:SV also served as a useful foil. Having a clear opponent typically makes organizing strong community sentiment easier, and while JV:SV was never actually a target for organizing campaigns – specific campaigns were organized around city and county government policy, or broad issue areas like a Children's Health Initiative or affordable housing – in community meetings and door-to-door organizing efforts, organizers could point to JV:SV as the "other" regional voice in the Valley. Surely, organizers argued, JV:SV should not be the only voice. This approach generated a sense of urgency around a counterpoint of community-based regional organizing and policy efforts.

Sometimes, the existence of business or policy-led regionalism hinders rather than helps the development of social movement regionalism. In Pittsburgh, for example, regional discussions have been dominated by the business-led Allegheny Conference on Community Development, whose focus over the past 20 years has primarily been on downtown revitalization and promotion of industries linked with the region's large educational and medical institutions. The Conference leaders combined their strong, organized connections to media outlets, regional politicians, and local funders with a paternal openness to CDC-oriented neighborhood groups. This cluster of power has marginalized more oppositional groups, making it difficult for them to gain traction in the public arena (Hamilton, 2004; Lubove, 1996; Pastor & Benner, 2008).

In comparison, the absence of effective business regionalism created an opening in Los Angeles. The relative weakness of business was most evident when the 1992 uprising exploded into the region's (and nation's) consciousness and led to the creation of Rebuild L.A. – which did little to mobilize corporate investment for the areas affected by the unrest. By the time it shut its doors five years later, it had shifted to a strategy of supporting small business development, reflecting the ongoing business fragmentation. With the field wide open, community organizers developed their own regional vision for lasting and far-reaching structural changes, including: the formation of the Los Angeles Alliance for a New Economy (LAANE) and its work on accountable development; the efforts of SCOPE to organize grassroots leadership in South Los Angeles and then link South LA to the rest of the region through their Metropolitan Alliance; the Bus Riders Union and its fight to improve transit for the region-wide working poor; and Strategic Actions for a Just Economy and its struggle to slow displacement and gentrification. As such, the 2005 mayoral election of progressive candidate Antonio Villaraigosa actually heralded a new era in which business had essentially ceded ground and realized that a social justice commitment would be the price they would have to pay to get support for large-scale regional economic investment and real-estate development.

Of course, absence of a strong business voice does not always make the social movement heart grow fonder. In the highly fragmented Detroit area, the Gamaliel organizers associated with MOSES have struggled to create a regional transportation authority and a single county-wide land bank. With few others, including business, pulling their weight at a regional scale, making the region come together is a challenge. Meanwhile, in northeast Ohio, the Fund for Our Economic Future has been paving a path toward regional revitalization that includes elements of social equity, having started their effort with a landmark study arguing that overcoming racial and income polarization was part of the competitiveness challenge; here, the worry has been that the equity-oriented regionalists are not quite ready to step up to the plate and the social justice agenda will be defined before they get there.

Business leaders can, to be sure, be indispensable allies for promoting particular regional equity strategies, especially housing and infrastructure-related ones. The Atlanta Neighborhood Development Partnership has sought to actively engage businesses, including lenders and developers, in their Mixed Income Communities Initiative. The Social Equity Caucus, which grew out of the Bay Area Alliance for Sustainable Communities, has collaborated with business on the Community Capital Investment Initiative and the Bay Area Family of Funds, both intended to promote Smart Growth development.

But it is, in our view, too easy to stress the "win–win" of undiscovered inner-city markets or find common (but shallow) ground on vaguely articulated principles of "inclusive development." In Los Angeles, for example, the now celebrated program called Workplace Hollywood – which reaches into inner-city communities to fill entertainment industry jobs – was only made possible because SCOPE led other groups in protesting a city subsidy going to DreamWorks to build a new studio. The protest led to tough negotiations and an agreement on job training – a commitment Dreamworks stuck by even when they decided not to build the studio, partly because of the relationships that had developed over the course of the fight. The collaboration grew from the conflict – and really moving the politics requires a sophisticated focus on how interests differ and intersect.

Social movement regionalists may be especially well-suited to this challenge. They tend to take into account market realities more than activists in other social movements – they know that business can make money *and* do good in underserved communities, and they understand that companies need to remain economically viable while also paying higher wages. But they also know that bringing people to the table sometimes requires protest and they are fundamentally about projecting a broader vision of economic possibilities. In this view, the community development focus on making deals and the policy reform emphasis on competitiveness can sometimes distract from the real prize: community power to influence regional outcomes.

### *Finding communities, bridging differences*

Community world-views may generally differ from business world-views, but they are neither singular nor homogeneous. Organizations may have a tight or a loose association to regional equity principles, or they may tend to focus more on projects, policies, or power. Bringing these perspectives under the same tent can often be a challenge.

This dynamic is particularly evident in a recent collaboration between Detroit LISC and MOSES. LISC is a classic example of a community-development approach to regionalism. Prior to 2002, Detroit LISC focused almost exclusively on traditional approaches to community development, assisting neighborhood revitalization primarily through helping community development corporations in their efforts to build affordable housing and revitalize commercial strips. By contrast, MOSES' very origins are rooted in some ways as a *reaction against* project-oriented community development. MOSES emerged from three previously existing neighborhood community development organizations that had separately been working to address quality-of-life issues through traditional community development processes, but were frustrated by their limited progress at the neighborhood scale. Since its founding in 1997, MOSES has been focusing on the broader processes undermining neighborhood revitalization initiatives, and stressing the need for regional power-building and democratic accountability.

According to MOSES organizers, Detroit LISC was a latecomer to regional equity – embracing regional strategies only in 2003, and yet garnering large amounts of attention and millions of dollars for work that essentially only modified traditional community-development approaches; LISC paid little attention to policy, advocacy, or power-building. Detroit LISC staff acknowledged both the organization's late start in implementing regional strategies and the fact that it had been prompted by external inspiration, both from National LISC and from the Ford Foundation. Yet they also argued that the nature of development work requires large amounts of money, and this led them to align themselves closely with banks and corporate economic development organizations. At times, they suggest, many people have viewed MOSES as being oppositional and obstructionist.

This seems a perfect setup for a conflict between community development and social movement regionalism. Yet MOSES and Detroit LISC were largely able to overcome many of these organizational and tactical differences. It may have helped that both groups were led by African American women working in environments historically dominated by men (church structures and financial/corporate institutions, respectively); this created a sense of shared experience and mutual understanding, and the two leaders were soon able to help their organizations find common ground, most importantly around efforts to develop a Land Bank in Detroit.

Even in cases where there is significant overlap in visions of regional equity, real tensions can surface. For example, when significant financial resources became available to engage in workforce training, the Campaign for a Sustainable Milwaukee (CSM), fundamentally an organizing effort founded by the Central Labor Council, joined forces with the Wisconsin Regional Training Partnership under the umbrella of the Milwaukee Jobs Initiative. The Milwaukee Jobs Initiative was a separate organization, but they subcontracted their training work to CSM – and CSM thought that it would be able to leverage its training service work to gain support for its organizing efforts. But it had difficultly doing so: the organizing and service components of CSM operated separately in practice, and people who received services were rarely substantially involved in the organizing efforts. With mission drift becoming mission split, CSM eventually collapsed.

One particularly difficult divide to bridge is often the divide between labor and community organizations. Labor/community alliances throughout the United States have generally been more the exception than the rule (for the exceptions, see Brecher and Costello, 1990). Part of this is due to the separation between residential space and workspace, which in turn contributes to the lack of connection between labor politics and community politics (Katznelson, 1981). In many contexts, the labor–community divide is reinforced through racial divides, particularly in the building trades, where people of color have often been excluded from the better paying union jobs. Labor-initiated "collaboration" has traditionally been limited to unions calling on community organizations for temporary support in particular organizing campaigns, or community organizations requesting labor's endorsement for particular initiatives.

Yet there has been a striking transformation, well-documented in Dean and Reynolds (2008), in the role of labor in community coalitions (see also Nissen, 2004; Rathke, 2004; Turner 2005). In Los Angeles and in San Jose, for example, much of the impetus for labor–community alliances came from the political process, and specifically in response to conservative-sponsored state-level initiatives around immigrant rights and restricting the political monies of unions. There is nothing quite like a shared battle to forge relationships and bring together unlikely allies, a form of "common cause coalitions" (Frege, Heery, & Turner, 2003). Community groups have come to understand the potential strength coming from unions and the value of maintaining ongoing union ties even as the unions have been able to demonstrate their commitment to a broader agenda. Over time, the coalition's relationships would intensify, morphing into an "integrative coalition" (Frege et al., 2003).

Leadership development and training programs have also been important for building strong labor–community ties. In San Jose, this took the form of a 12-week Leadership Institute (mentioned earlier) that brings together key constituencies in an applied, leadership development program; in Los Angeles, the Community Scholars Program at UCLA serves a similar function. Jointly sponsored by the Department of Urban Planning and the Center for Labor Research and Education, the program brings labor and community leaders together for a two-quarter-long academic and training program focused on specific community development issues in the region: topics have ranged from popular education, to banking in communities, to the impact of Walmart. The very first program in 1991/92 focused on Los Angeles' tourism industry and played a critical role in the founding of the Tourism Industry Development Corporation, the predecessor to LAANE. Similar to Working Partnerships Leadership Institute, the Community Scholars Program has broken down barriers between labor and community groups by convening labor and community leaders together in a shared environment to study and develop solutions to regional problems.

Of course, relations between labor and community groups in even these "success stories" have their problems. Stressors continue to exist, rooted in a range of issues including different organizational structures, unequal power, different constituencies, and sometimes, conflicting goals. Community groups, in particular, remain wary of labor's power – while unions may seem toothless compared with business, they are an overwhelming force for many smaller community groups. Yet in many metropolitan areas, labor and community groups have moved beyond coming together only around specific campaigns or fashioning coalitions whose sole aim is to achieve discrete outcomes. Through ongoing, long-term communication and collaboration, labor and community groups have networked together to form a dense "civic infrastructure" with a mutual understanding of regional programs and a sense of inter-dependency.

The tensions between equity agendas, between organizing and implementation, and between labor and community groups do not necessarily result in groups abandoning their regional collaborative work. Detroit LISC and MOSES see their futures as intertwined, and they continue to find ways to collaborate when possible. Many members of the former Campaign for a Sustainable Milwaukee remain active in the Good Jobs and Livable Neighborhoods Coalition, and see the more programmatic work of the Wisconsin Regional Training Partnership as an essential part of retaining and building a strong political base in the region. Labor and community groups have found ongoing ways to work together in San Jose and Los Angeles. In many ways, it is the regional economic and political processes that provide these groups with a way of navigating the tensions of different ideological perspectives and varying organizational activities.

*Reaching across race*

Perhaps the single most important issue simmering in the regional equity world is race. On the one hand, racial inequity and segregation have been key factors in creating the unequal metropolitan landscape of America – and many early leaders in the regional equity movement, be they white, black, Latino, Asian, or other, cut their organizing teeth on some variant of the civil rights movement. On the other hand, the effort to find commonalities across city and suburb, rich and poor, white and minority, has sometimes led to a fuzzy politics that sets aside or diffuses issues of race to build regional coalitions or work on specific issues (e.g. transportation, housing, smart growth, etc.).

Consider the Detroit–Grosse Pointe Park Collaborative, a city-suburb neighborhood revitalization effort on Detroit's eastern border that has been sponsored by LISC as part of its own regional efforts. The contrast between black and white could hardly be more stark: Gross Pointe Park was developed as an exclusive suburb, housing wealthy executives and managers from Detroit's auto firms, and in 2000 the city's population was 93% white and 60% college-educated, with an annual median household income over $80,000. In the adjacent Detroit community, the population was nearly 90% African American, only 9% college-educated, and the annual median household income was $25,020. Despite the evident disparities, both white and black organizers from the initiative chose *not* to focus on these differences in their organizing efforts. Instead, they organized around building a cross-border neighborhood business association and fostering communication through sports leagues and other recreational activities for children, in an attempt to bring blacks and whites together without talking about racial differences.

Compare this strategy with that used by the Wisconsin Regional Training Partnership to organize workers within the construction industry in Milwaukee. Here, the historic racial inequalities are also quite stark: well-paying unionized construction jobs were largely reserved for white men, and people of color were largely excluded from the building trades and relegated to lower-paid laborer positions (Butler, 2006; Waldinger & Bailey, 1991). Yet in the late 1990s, union leaders recognized the intersection of two major trends. First, the level of unionization in the construction trades was declining across the board; second, increasing numbers of Latino immigrants and African Americans were being employed by the industry, often in non-unionized jobs.

To capitalize on these trends and rebuild union strength, leaders sought to leverage labor agreements on projects involving direct public expenditures or subsidies and concurrently reaching out to minority constituencies. To succeed, they had to credibly demonstrate their commitment to expanding diversity in both the rank-and-file and the leadership of construction unions. They established trust by investing significant amounts of time and resources into BIG STEP, a pre-apprenticeship program for inner-city African American residents, designed to provide pathways into the better paying apprenticeship programs in the building trades. In essence, attention to race and historical patterns of racial discrimination became central to their regional organizing strategies.

The question of how much to emphasize race and racial differences in American politics is not unique to the regional equity movement – indeed, it runs through nearly every aspect of policy-making and coalition-building in this country. Yet it is a particularly sharp tension in this arena precisely because America's urban form – struggling central cities and isolated suburbs – is in many ways the physical manifestation of highly racialized processes of segregation. Race, in short, is an inescapable part of America's regional histories and racism a part of its social institutions.

Talking about race is difficult – both for whites who may be uncomfortable with the implication that they benefit from unfair privileges, and for people of color who are tired of being seen only through the prism of their ethnicity. In large part, the conversation about race revolves around political power – who has it, who does not, and what it will take to get it (Thompson, 2002). In some sense, regional equity tries to complicate this dimension. It celebrates Richard Hatcher of Gary, Indiana, for becoming the first African American mayor of a large US city – but it also notes that he inherited a deindustrializing economy that deprived Gary of its resources and left it with a shrinking public-sector capacity to address the increasing social and economic needs of its people. Regional equity proponents thus argue for a focus on the regional economic common ground – but it seems clear that we cannot build up the economic capacity of the inner city without also addressing the visibility and viability of inner-city political leadership as well (Thompson, 2005).

This effort to simultaneously embrace regional common ground and address historical political discrimination leads to contradictions in the support bases for regionalism. Since so much of the regional equity agenda could benefit disadvantaged areas, many, particularly in the policy reform camp, assume that there will be a natural constituency for regional equity in communities of color. Yet many of these same communities have long been suspicious of regionalism, particularly in places where minority political power stems from geographic concentration; higher levels of regional governance are seen as potentially diluting hard-won political voice. In Louisville, Kentucky, for example, the African American community was largely opposed to a city–county merger for exactly that reason. In Cleveland, Ohio, African American leaders perceived regionalism as being primarily driven by white suburban communities (Savitch & Vogel, 2004). In the racially charged atmosphere of Camden, New Jersey, regional equity efforts have sometimes been perceived as a way to drain the city of residents or pit the inner ring suburbs against Camden.

Highly segregated Detroit provides a compelling example of one way to overcome this challenge. With few opportunities for whites and blacks to interact in their neighborhoods, building cross-racial organizations requires conscious effort.

Patrick Gahegan, a white pastor in a predominantly African American congregation in the City of Detroit and one of the leading pastors within MOSES, describes the dynamic:

> Initially, I didn't get involved with Moses ... In this divided region, [when I was first exposed to the organization] MOSES was seen as a white organization and couldn't cut it in the black community ... at the time [1998] the organizers were all white. Gamaliel itself was perceived as all white. That is still the perception in most of the black churches ... In the suburbs, MOSES is seen as a black organization. It is all relative. Detroiters aren't used to walking in a room and seeing half white and half black. That is out of the context of what goes on here. African Americans see all the white people and say this is a white organization. White folks see all the African Americans and say this is a black organization ... the leadership of MOSES ... have helped address this, but the truth is that Detroit has become so polarized. It is who we are. It is built into the DNA of us as a people. (Benner, 2006)

To overcome these historic racial divisions, MOSES built an organization with congregations throughout the Detroit Metro region. These congregations are sometimes predominantly African American and sometimes predominantly white. For them, focusing on metropolitan equity has become a means of overcoming racial divides. Through their relentless organizing, they have started to forge a sense of shared destiny between white and black residents of the region.

The challenges are different in the multi-racial metros like those in California. In both Los Angeles and the Bay Area, whites no longer represent a majority of the population, and have not for years. With rapid growth in the Latino population and large numbers of Asian residents, both regions truly reflect a demographic tapestry of race and ethnicities. While white/non-white tensions are still important, there are also important tensions across the range of races and ethnicities. African American neighborhoods in South Los Angeles and East Palo Alto (Silicon Valley), for instance, have experienced a rapid influx of Latino immigrants, resulting in rising tensions that have sometimes exploded into violence. Korean communities in Los Angeles and Vietnamese communities in San Jose face particular challenges associated with being smaller enclaves in a wider urban context (Martinez Jr & Valenzuela Jr, 2006).

But with all the talk of race, we are especially struck by lessons from the election of Antonio Villaraigosa, the first Latino mayor in Los Angeles in over 130 years. His victory was partly driven by regional equity proponents who had worked to win landmark community benefits agreements, build a new metropolitan labor movement, and change the politics of the city and the region – and his field campaign in 2005 was actually run by the head of SCOPE, Anthony Thigpenn. Villaraigosa was perceived as an effective advocate for racial justice, partly because of his previous positions in public life and partly because he invested campaign time and resources to bring together African American and Latino constituencies. But despite his commitment to racial equality, he downplayed race in his campaign, instead lifting up common aspirations for education, public safety, and economic betterment, and running on a regionalist platform derived from a period spent at the Southern California Studies Center at USC. His mantra, adopted from his time there, was about the city needing to "grow smarter, grow safer, grow greener, grow together, and grow more civic-minded" (Fulton, 2003, p. 8).

In short, Villaraigosa's run for mayor embodied the tension of the regional equity movement – the need to have credibility on issues of race while crafting a vision and policy package that can create broad agreement and a sense of common destiny. It is not an easy balance, but it is the one that needs to be struck if America's racialized metropolitan landscape is to be altered for a more inclusive future, and social movement regionalists have a particularly astute sense of how to strike this balance.

**Scaling on up**

Regional equity is fundamentally about scale – the proponents are insisting that the problems are caused at the regional level, that policies to address these should focus on the regional level, and that the power analysis and power-building that can change things might be most usefully pursued at a regional level. But another aspect of all this is whether one can scale up from the region – connecting not just actors within a metro but also actors across America's metros – to actually influence and drive national politics.

To some extent, all the variants of regional equity have national aspirations. Community developers are seeking to rework the field, and policy entrepreneurs are hoping that a new administration will once again allow metropolitan experiments to find federal support. The social movement regionalists, we would suggest, have a different ambition: like their conservative counterparts who changed the politics of America by working their way from the school boards of Kansas to the halls of Congress, many are hoping to build a new progressive politics for America one community-benefits agreement, one city–suburb alliance, one transit equity initiative at a time.

The Gamaliel Foundation, a prime example and the network to which MOSES belongs, has adopted metropolitan equity as a central organizing lens and works to promote this perspective throughout its network of 60 affiliates in 21 states. The Partnership for Working Families, a network spanning 18 affiliates in 10 states, including LAANE and Working Partnerships, has developed a new model for urban growth and social justice that analyzes regional sources of inequality and utilizes community benefits agreements as an organizing tool. The Transportation Equity Network, originally founded under the aegis of the Center for Community Change, has brought together organizations such as the Bus Riders Union (Los Angeles), the Northwest Interfaith Federation (Northwest Indiana), the Metropolitan Congregations United (Missouri), and West Harlem Environmental Action (New York) (Swanstrom & Barrett, 2007). The Right to the City Alliance brings together groups around the country, including Strategic Actions for a Just Economy and the Miami Workers Center, who are fighting gentrification by equating their power-building efforts with regional equity goals and a human rights framing. The Pushback Network, with organizations from eight states, including SCOPE in Los Angeles, links and builds capacity of progressive grassroots organizing efforts focused on electoral strategies and state alliance building.

These are big ambitions but they come at a time when the country does seem ripe for change. People are looking for a new policy framework, to be sure, but they are also looking for a new narrative that brings together a disparate nation. The regional equity strategy – in which relationships are negotiated face to face, place to place, and race to race – offers an entry into a new conversation. Moreover, the lessons learned at the regional level are instructive in another way: navigating between the Scylla of a mythical conflict-free "kumbaya" coalition for justice, and the Charybdis of divisive and conflictual politics of blame, social movement regionalists are finding ways of dealing with conflict in productive ways. By not shying away from confronting power, but also building a sense of common destiny, social movement regionalists are pointing the way towards a forward-looking and practical vision that can have a real impact on America's regions and maybe America itself.

We have no naiveté about the challenges they face at either the regional or national level. Maintaining credibility on race while crafting a vision and a policy package that can create consensus, drawing the connection between regional issues while highlighting neighborhood distresses, balancing the need to agitate for justice with the desire to attract private capital, dealing with fragmentation by jurisdiction, geography, and politics – these are just some of the difficulties regional equity activists juggle. We get tired just listing them; organizers seem tireless in tackling them.

But we are still optimistic. Two of us met for the first time in a church in South Central Los Angeles nearly a decade ago. One of us was a graduate student and the other had recently authored a report on connecting communities and regions. The author was there to provide some academic testimony for the effort to challenge DreamWorks; the graduate student was providing research for the campaign. We both offered facts, charts, and admonitions about a new regional approach – then a local preacher, in a far more effective approach, called the congregants to understand the moral imperative at hand. In a lilting cadence, he invoked "people are tired of drifting apart, they want to be growing together!"

Who was to know that this message would take off, resonating with the central labor councils that have pushed for accountable development, the churches and community groups that have struggled for transportation justice, and the long-time residents who are working against gentrification? They have gone beyond projects and policy, using regional equity as a new terrain for transformative politics. Understanding the challenges these social movements face, documenting the choices they make, and celebrating the spirits they lift should be the focus of the next phase of research in this field. There is, after all, something happening here.

**References**

Anglin, R.V., & Montezemolo, S.C. (2004). *Supporting the community development movement: The achievements and challenges of intermediary organizations*. Washington, DC: US Department of Housing and Urban Development.
Benner, C. (2006). *Interview with Patrick Gahegan*, Detroit, MI, February 2.
Brecher, J., & Costello, T. 1990. *Building bridges: The emerging coalition of labor and community*. New York: Monthly Review Press.
Butler, G. (2006). *Disunited brotherhoods: Race, racketeering and the fall of the New York construction unions*. Lincoln, NB: iUniverse.
Dean, A.B., & Reynolds, D.B. (2008). Labor's new regional strategy: The rebirth of central labor councils. *New Labor Forum*, 17(1), 46–55.
Frege, C., Heery, E., & Turner, L. (2003). Comparative coalition building and the revitalization of the labor movement. Paper presented at the Industrial Relations Research Association Conference, Washington, DC, 3–5 January.
Fulton, W., Wolch, J., Villaraigosa, A., & Weaver, S. (2003). *After sprawl: Action plans for metropolitan Los Angeles*. Los Angeles: Southern California Studies Center, University of Southern California.
Gordon, A. (2008). A victory for affordable housing in N.J. *Next American City*, July 21. Retrieved from http://americancity.org/daily/entry/943/
Hamilton, D. (2004). Developing regional regimes: A comparison of two metropolitan areas. *Journal of Urban Affairs*, 26(4), 455–477.

Imbroscio, D. (2006). Shaming the inside game: A critique of the liberal expansionist approach to addressing urban problems. *Urban Affairs Review*, *42*(224), 248.

Jonas, A.E.G., & Pincetl, S. (2006). Rescaling regions in the state: The new regionalism in California. *Political Geography*, *25*, 482–505.

Jones, M., & MacLeod, G. (2004). Regional spaces, spaces of regionalism: Territory, insurgent politics and the English question. *Transactions of the Institute of British Geographers*, *29*(4), 433–452.

Katznelson, I. (1981). *City trenches: Urban politics and the patterning of class in the United States*. Chicago: University of Chicago Press.

Kleidman, R. (2004). Community organizing and regionalism. *City and Community*, *3*(4), 403–421.

Lubove, R. (1996). *Twentieth century Pittsburgh: Volume 2, the post steel era*. Pittsburgh: University of Pittsburgh Press.

Martinez Jr, R., & Valenzuela Jr, A. (Eds.). (2006). *Immigration and crime: Ethnicity, race and violence*. New York: New York University Press.

Mintrom, M. (1997). Policy entrepreneurs and the diffusion of innovation. *American Journal of Political Science*, *41*(3), 738–770.

Nissen, B. (2004). The effectiveness and limits of labor-community coalitions: Evidence from South Florida. *Labor Studies Journal*, *29*(1), 67–89.

Pastor, M. (2006). Cohesion and competitiveness: Business leadership for regional growth and social equity. In *OECD territorial reviews, competitive cities in the global economy*. Paris, France: Organisation for Economic Co-Operation and Development, 393–445.

Pastor, M., & Benner, C. (2008). Been down so long: Week market cities and regional equity. In R. McGahey & J. Vey (Eds.), *Restoring prosperity in older industrial areas*. Washington, DC: Brookings Institution Press, 89–118.

Pastor, M., Benner, C., & Matsuoka, M. (2009). *This could be the start of something big: Regional equity organizing and the future of metropolitan America*. Ithaca, NY: Cornell University Press.

Pastor, M., Benner, C., & Rosner, R. (2006). *Edging toward equity: Creating shared opportunity in America's regions*. Santa Cruz, CA: Center for Justice Tolerance and Community: UCSC.

Pastor, M., Dreier, P., Grigsby, R., & Garza, M.L. (2000). *Regions that work: How cities and suburbs can grow together*. Minneapolis: University of Minnesota Press.

Rathke, W. (2004). Majority unionism: Strategies for organizing the 21st century labor movement. *Social Policy*, *35*(1), 18–30.

Roberts, N.C., & King, P.J. (1991). Policy entrepreneurs: Their activity structure and function in the policy process. *Journal of Public Administration Research and Theory*, *1*(2), 147–155.

Rusk, D. (1999). *Inside game outside game: Winning strategies for saving urban America*. Washington, DC: Brookings Institution Press.

Savitch, H.V., & Vogel, R.K. (2004). Suburbs without a city: Power and city-county consolidation. *Urban Affairs Review*, *39*, 758–90.

Swanstrom, T., & Barrett, L. (2007). The road to jobs: The fight for transportation equity. *Social Policy*, spring and Summer. Retrieved from http://www.socialpolicy.org/index.php?id=1833

Thompson, J.P. (2002). Review of place matters: Metropolitics for the Twenty-First Century by Peter Dreier, John Mollenkopf, and Todd Swanstrom (Lawrence: University Press of Kansas). *Urban Affairs*, *37*, 442–451.

Thompson, J.P. (2005). Seeking effective power: Why mayors need community organizations. *Perspectives on Politics*, *3*, 301–308.

Turner, L. (2005). From transformation to revitalization: A new research agenda for a contested global economy. *Work and Occupations*, *32*, 383–399.

Waldinger, R., & Bailey, T. (1991). The continuing significance of race: Racial conflict and racial discrimination in construction *Politics & Society*, *19*, 291–323.

Walsh, J. (1997). *Stories of renewal: Community building and the future of urban America*. New York: The Rockefeller Foundation.

Weir, M., & Rongerude, J. (2007). *Multi-level power and progressive regionalism. MacArthur Foundation research network on building resilient regions*. Working Paper. Berkeley, CA: UC Berkeley, Institute of Urban and Regional Development.

Weir, M., Rongerude, J., & Ansell, C.K. (2007). *Collaboration is not enough. MacArthur Foundation Research Network on building resilient regions*. Working Paper. Institute of Urban and Regional Development. Berkeley: University of California, Berkeley.

Wilton, R.D., & Cranford, C. (2002). Toward an understanding of the spatiality of social movements: Labor organizing at a private university in Los Angeles. *Social Problems, 49*(3), 374–394.

Young, I.M. (2000). *Inclusion and democracy*. Cambridge: Oxford University Press.

# Spatial justice through regionalism? The inside game, the outside game, and the quest for the spatial fix in the United States

Karen Chapple[a] and Edward G. Goetz[b]

[a]*City & Regional Planning, UC-Berkeley, Berkeley, California, USA;* [b]*University of Minnesota, Twin Cities, Minneapolis, Minnesota, USA*

> Some regionalists advocate a spatial fix for urban poverty by engaging suburbs in a regional solution. This paper analyzes three such regionalist strategies in light of theories of justice. The idea behind regional strategies for poverty is that they will allow for equality of opportunity and thus improve the life-chances of the impoverished. Yet, casting justice in terms of equality of opportunity alone means neglecting the non-economic aspects of life – capabilities, social needs, urban life and vitality. Changing the spatial distribution of the population may create a more optimal and equitable spatial allocation, but in some ways it fails to acknowledge basic human aspirations to live in security, in community, or in a revitalized core.

Taake my word for it Sammy, the poor in a loomp is bad. (Tennyson's *The Northern Farmer* quoted in Lund, 1999)

## 1. Introduction

In the 1960s, US social scientists began a protracted debate about the causes of and remedies for urban poverty, a discussion that accelerated in the 1980s with the realization that new concentrations of poverty were developing. As the poverty research industry matured, it emphasized the role of contagion effects of place and the behavior of the poor in causing poverty, to the exclusion of macro-economic, structural factors (O'Connor, 2001). Moreover, researchers and policy-makers increasingly saw federal solutions to urban poverty as politically nonviable, due not only to a growing climate of devolution and neoliberalism, but also because of high-profile public policy disasters such as public housing. In this context, a new set of regional strategies to address poverty and inequity emerged by the 1990s, a movement alternatively called "new regionalism," or, more narrowly, "equity regionalism," "regional equity," or "progressive regionalism" (Bollens, 2003; Brenner, 2002). These strategies propose to engage the suburbs in solving the problem of urban poverty, typically through either structural changes to remedy fiscal inequity between city and suburb, or spatial solutions that open up suburban housing or jobs to the urban poor.

The equity regionalist program grows out of the initial awareness of urban–suburban disparity powerfully articulated by the Kerner Commission in 1968, with its warning that "Our nation is moving toward two societies, one black, one white – separate and unequal." The primary cause, as supported by research by John Kain (1992), was the shift of new employment opportunities to the suburbs and the lack of federal policies to connect urban residents, particularly African Americans, to jobs; the major remedy was to be opening up the suburbs to the disadvantaged. This early framing of the urban poverty problem as connected to urban–suburban disparities quickly became the prevailing wisdom. By the mid-1990s, researchers were framing the problem in terms of the "geography of metropolitan opportunity," referring to the actual prospects that the opportunity structure (as governed by markets, institutions, and social systems) offers based on geography (Galster & Killen, 1995). In another memorable construction, Rusk (1999) analogized the landscape of metropolitan opportunity to the game of basketball, prescribing a focus on the outside game as the way to solve the problems of the inside game.

Regional strategies to remedy unequal opportunity include reducing tax or service disparities (typically either via tax base sharing or new regional governing strategies) or changing the spatial distribution of population (for instance through creating new housing choices in the suburbs, moving inner-city residents to the suburbs, or transporting city residents to suburban jobs). Although the former set of policies arguably offered the most potential (Altshuler et al., 1999; Orfield, 1997), the spatial accessibility policies have dominated the policy and planning dialogue since the 1990s – and thus are the focus herein.

Two types of regional accessibility strategies might help overcome the economic and social isolation of the inner city. The first (called the "dispersal strategy" by Hughes, 1995) helps urban residents move to the suburbs by spurring more suburban affordable housing construction through fair share housing policies, providing Section 8 vouchers, and/or helping to overcome housing discrimination. The second (called the "mobility strategy") uses transportation improvements to connect disadvantaged urban residents more effectively to jobs in the suburbs. The focus of these strategies is to improve access to the resources or opportunities of the region's outer rings, to create a more just spatial distribution.

Members of the accessibility camp of equity regionalism self-identify as advocates of social justice. The idea behind dispersal and mobility strategies for poverty is essentially just: they will allow for equality of opportunity and thus improve the life-chances of the impoverished. These equity regionalists implicitly seek to maximize individual utility, seeing mobility as the means – in what Imbroscio (2006) calls the mode of "liberal expansionism." The need to level the playing field creates an imperative for action; as a National Academy of Sciences committee on metropolitan governance framed it: "A lack of equal opportunity is thus in the most profound sense a 'moral' problem for Americans" (Altshuler et al., 1999, p. 18).

Yet, a growing body of work on the "just city" (for example, Fainstein, 2006; Nussbaum, 2000; Sen, 1999) implies that regional accessibility strategies to address poverty may not address systemic injustices. Although remedying unequal opportunity is obviously important to regional equity, it may not be possible to satisfy common aspirations and respect human dignity through policy that attempts to construct an even landscape of metropolitan opportunity by rearranging the population. Planners adopting liberal conceptions of justice embrace an abstract principle of equality at the expense of situated ethical judgment that appreciates individual circumstance (Campbell, 2006).

This paper examines the idea and practice of regional anti-poverty strategies in the light of different conceptions of social justice. We begin by describing regional accessibility strategies – fair share housing, other dispersal policies, and mobility programs – and their outcomes thus far. We then show how these policies find their moral underpinnings in the work of Rawls (1971). We next examine alternative notions of social justice; in particular, the ideas of capabilities, the need for affiliation, and the "right to the city" and urban life (Lefebvre, 1996; Nussbaum, 2000; Sen, 1999). We conclude by discussing whether and how the state and planners can intervene to produce a more just metro for those living in concentrated poverty neighborhoods.

## 2. Overview of regional accessibility strategies and their outcomes

Throughout the twentieth century, regionalists advanced spatial strategies to improve regional efficiency and competitiveness, with notable examples from the 1929 Regional Plan of New York to the advent of regional councils of government and metropolitan planning organizations in the 1960s and 1970s, to plans such as *Envision Utah!* in the 1990s. The push for equity regionalism emerged relatively late in the game, as awareness of urban–suburban disparities increased. Fair share housing programs (including inclusionary zoning), which require developers to provide low-income or moderate-income housing units in exchange for development permission, were implemented by multiple states in the 1970s (Listokin, 1976). The 1970s saw some trials of dispersal and mobility programs, but it was not until the 1990s that the federal government implemented larger-scale experiments. The following provides an overview of these policies and their successes and failures.

### 2.1. Fair share housing

Regional fair share housing strategies attempt to address inequities in the regional distribution of affordable housing, in order to shift more affordable housing provision to the outside game (Bollens, 2003; Listokin, 1976). Typically, the approach is based on a formula for assigning affordable housing obligations to regional sub-areas, most frequently individual municipalities within a single metropolitan area. The formulae can take different forms, emphasizing a range of parameters that can be used to establish what a "fair" distribution of housing opportunities within a metro area should look like. Typical elements of fair share formulae are the existing population in sub-areas, estimated population growth, and the (inverse of) relative availability of low-cost or subsidized housing. In more sophisticated models, constraints on development such as jobs, job growth, and transportation accessibility are incorporated (see Goetz & Flack, 2008).

The fair share approach was popular in the United States for a short period of time more than 30 years ago. In the early 1970s, shortly after passage of the Fair Housing Act, the US Department of Housing and Urban Development supported the creation of fair share strategies in metro areas around the country. Regional authorities in a number of areas created programs aimed at producing a more equitable distribution of subsidized housing between cities and their suburban satellites. These efforts, and the US Department of Housing and Urban Development's interest in supporting them, were short-lived.

Probably the best of these programs, the Regional Housing Needs Assessment process in California, has survived largely due to the threat of litigation. Although it has undeniably raised awareness of the need for affordable housing among California's communities, it has compromised in its commitment to affordability (Calavita, Grimes, & Mallach, 1997). In other places, the rapid decline in federal subsidies for low-cost housing has rendered fair share allocation systems irrelevant by making the development of affordable housing difficult in *all* communities. Further, the lack of political appetite for subsidized housing in the suburbs has been an insurmountable obstacle to implementation of fair share schemes (Basolo & Hastings, 2003; Goetz, 2003; Goetz, Chapple, & Lukermann, 2003). In Minnesota's fair share housing program, a lack of funding, political will, and planner savvy meant that just five acres of every 100 acres set aside for affordable housing in the program actually had new low-income or moderate-income housing 20 years later (Goetz et al., 2003).

One of the few programs to endure was the court-ordered effort in New Jersey. A product of the *Mt. Laurel I* and *Mt. Laurel II* rulings, the state of New Jersey produced a system of regional fair share housing administered by the statewide Council on Affordable Housing. In place for more than 20 years, this program imposes an affirmative obligation on communities within urban regions to create affordable housing. Over 22,000 units of housing were subsidized in the first 10 years of the program (Wish & Eisdorfer, 1997). The potential for the program to significantly alter the spatial distribution of low-cost housing is seriously limited by the program provision that allows municipalities to purchase compliance credits from each other. Under these so-called Regional Contribution Agreements, a community that does not wish to actually build affordable housing can transfer up to 50% of its affordable housing obligation to another community by paying the second community. The receiving community – typically larger, lower-income, and more racially diverse communities – take, in the aggregate, millions of dollars from higher-income, whiter communities to finance affordable housing efforts.

The scale of the New Jersey approach is sufficient to produce a sizable number of affordable housing units in communities that probably would not have built them otherwise. In this respect, the program is producing a more equitable distribution of housing opportunities within the state's urban regions (notwithstanding the limiting effects of Regional Contribution Agreements). However, in terms of facilitating a movement of families out of concentrated poverty, or out of racially segregated areas, the program has had a negligible effect. Most units built in the suburban areas of metro regions are occupied by families who already lived in the suburbs. Only 6.8% of units are occupied by African-American families who moved out of a central city and into a suburb. When movement in the other direction is accounted for (i.e. the movement of African-American families out of the suburbs and into a Mt. Laurel unit built within a central city), the net movement of such families into desegregated suburban areas accounts for less than 2% of all Mt. Laurel units (Wish & Eisdorfer, 1997).

Related to the fair share housing approach is inclusionary zoning (IZ), which mandates construction of affordable units, typically on-site within new housing developments. Although most IZ programs are implemented at the city level, there is one notable exception: Montgomery County's Moderately Priced Dwelling Unit

Ordinance. This ordinance, which passed in 1973, mandates that 15% of the units in new subdivisions be affordable, and further makes one-third of these available for purchase by the county's public housing authority. Unlike fair share housing programs, the Montgomery County ordinance is widely considered successful, although small scale (with just 11,000 units built over 30 years) (PolicyLink, 2004; Rusk, 1999). However, other regions have lacked the political will, the strong market, and/or the resources to replicate the program. Moreover, like most of the other fair share programs, regional IZ is not creating a new even landscape of opportunity: it cannot facilitate a large-scale relocation of the urban poor, not only because of its small scale but also because it typically fails to provide much very low-income housing.

## 2.2. Dispersal programs

Dispersal policy is reflected in three major policy initiatives: the Gautreaux program, Moving To Opportunity, and the HOPE VI program. The Gautreaux consent decree – which was followed by others in at least 11 metropolitan areas – forced the Chicago Housing Authority to develop a "metropolitan-wide 'mobility program'" to partially compensate for its discriminatory practice of placing public housing in predominantly African-American or racially changing areas (Goetz, 2003, p. 53). Over a 20-year period, more than 7100 families were relocated from virtually all-black urban areas to middle-income, overwhelmingly white areas in Chicago and its suburbs (Rubinowitz & Rosenbaum, 2000).

Inspired by the success of Gautreaux and its tenant-based mobility structure, Congress authorized the Moving to Opportunity (MTO) demonstration program in 1992 in the cities of Baltimore, Boston, Chicago, Los Angeles, and New York City. Participants in an experimental group (which was paired with two control groups) moved from very high-poverty to low-poverty neighborhoods. MTO, then, was an early attempt to assess whether low-poverty areas translated into improved life-chances for low-income households. These improvements would come in part from improved access to jobs, better schools for children, and the development of social capital, particularly in the form of social support and leverage provided by social ties and community institutions (Briggs, 1998; Clampet-Lundquist, 2007; Wexler, 2001).

As with other deconcentration programs, HOPE VI, authorized in 1992, involved the relocation of residents of distressed public housing to different neighborhoods. HOPE VI provides funds to local housing authorities for the redevelopment of severely distressed public housing projects. HOPE VI projects typically involve displacement and relocation of public housing residents, and demolition to make way for newly constructed, mixed-income developments. It differs from Gautreaux and MTO in its larger scope, involving both demolition and construction, and much larger scale, since hundreds of public housing authorities nationwide have implemented it.

Program outcomes have generally been mixed, with voluntary programs like MTO faring slightly better than involuntary like HOPE VI. Most prominently, no dispersal policy has had a demonstrable positive effect on economic opportunity, as measured by employment, earnings, or income of individuals. In the Gautreaux program in Chicago, the outcome for families who moved to the suburbs was no change in employment or wages (Rosenbaum & Popkin, 1991). This failure is repeated for individuals in the MTO program, every HOPE VI study thus far completed, and even the US Department of Housing and Urban Development's Welfare to Work Voucher Program (Clampet-Lundquist, 2004; Curley 2006; Goering & Feins, 2003; Goetz, 2002; Levy & Woolley, 2007; Kling, Liebman, & Katz, 2007; Rubinowitz & Rosenbaum, 2000; Popkin, Rosenbaum, & Meaden, 1993; Turney, Clampet-Lundquist, Edin, Kling, & Duncan, 2006). Dispersal may actually increase economic insecurity: relocatees lack money for food and rent and lack residential stability (Barrett, Geisel, & Johnston, 2006; Buron, Popkin, Levy, Harris, & Khadduri, 2002; Buron, Levy, & Gallagher, 2007; Clampet-Lundquist, 2004; Gibson, 2007; Popkin, 2006; Reed & Steinberg, 2006).

Although initial findings from the Gautreaux experiment suggested that relocating to the suburbs would have a positive outcome on schooling, subsequent studies have tempered those results, and effects on achievement overall seem to be small (Gallagher & Bajaj, 2007; Kaufman & Rosenbaum, 1992; Kling & Liebman, 2004; Popkin, 2006; Sanbonmatsu, Kling, Duncan, & Brooks-Gunn, 2006). The majority of studies also show little in the way of a health benefit for low-income individuals (Clampet-Lundquist, Edin, Kling, & Duncan, 2006; Gallagher & Bajaj, 2007; Kling & Liebman, 2004; Manjarrez, Popkin, & Guernsey, 2007; Popkin, 2006). The move itself seems to have negative impacts on those forced to relocate (e.g. in HOPE VI), because of their attachment to place (Kleit & Manzo, 2006; Gibson, 2007).

Perhaps most important, relocation does not seem to build social capital or stimulate social interaction between higher-income and lower-income residents (Barrett et al., 2006; Clampet-Lundquist, 2004, 2007; Goetz, 2003). Individuals who had relied on friends or other local connections to gain employment when they lived in the (pre-HOPE VI) public housing development did not report using the same techniques after moving to new neighborhoods (Clampet-Lundquist, 2004). Movers find less supportive neighbors and may even encounter resistance from locals (Curley, 2006; Greenbaum, Hathaway, Rodrigez, Spalding, & Ward, 2008; Goetz, 2003; Kleit & Manzo, 2006). Recent work on diversity (Putnam, 2007) supports this finding: communities may be coping with their diversity by avoiding high levels of interaction.

On the plus side, studies consistently show that families that move out of neighborhoods of concentrated poverty report benefits of increased sense of safety (see Buron et al. 2002; Gibson, 2007; Goetz, 2003; Popkin & Cove, 2007). Moreover, improvements in housing and neighborhood characteristics consistently occur (Brooks, Zugazaga, Wolk, & Adams, 2005; Buron et al., 2002; Comey, 2007; Curley, 2006; Kleit & Manzo, 2006; Gallagher & Bajaj, 2007; Gibson, 2007; Goetz, 2003; Popkin, 2006; Popkin et al., 2004). Yet, weighed against the disadvantages of relocation, it is difficult to make a case that these benefits add up to improvements in opportunity for the disadvantaged.

What happens to the urban neighborhoods and housing projects left behind? Studies have not examined systematically what happens to communities that have experienced exits from their public housing stock via consent decrees or MTO. But there is growing evidence that HOPE VI developments result in increases in property values (and presumably, gentrification) in the surrounding neighborhoods (Bair & Fitzgerald, 2005; Zielenbach, 2003). This outcome may be positive or negative: some homeowners will benefit from the housing price appreciation, and residents generally will enjoy improved access to services and amenities – but renters may not be able to stay in the area as rents increase, and some homeowners may not be able to afford the higher property taxes that come with new assessments.

## 2.3. Mobility programs

Another major approach to make jobs more accessible is to connect jobseekers to opportunities throughout the metropolitan region through transportation, under the assumption that job accessibility is a major barrier to employment. Most funding to link low-income urban residents to suburban jobs (for instance, the Jobs Access and Reverse Commute program) has supported reverse commuting via transit or vanpooling; more recently, programs have experimented with low-income auto ownership.

Historically, such initiatives have had little success, particularly in terms of reducing inner-city unemployment, although they may help those who are already employed (Crain, 1970; O'Regan & Quigley, 1999; Rosenbloom, 1992). This failure was repeated in the recent Bridges to Work experiment, which provided job placement and transportation services to help urban low-skilled workers access suburban jobs in five regions. This approach did not increase employment or earnings (compared with a control group) (Roder & Scrivner, 2005). Perhaps because the labor market was relatively tight when the program was implemented, turnover at the suburban jobs was high; given the choice between the low-wage, low-skill jobs in the suburbs or close to home in the city, jobseekers chose the latter. Workers will not choose long reverse commutes if they cannot realize substantially higher wages in return. The findings indicated that workforce development, particularly recruitment and job-readiness, is the major policy challenge in improving the employment chances of the disadvantaged, rather than spatial mismatch. The lack of financial compensation for long commutes makes the idea of a truly regional labor market unrealistic for many, if not most, disadvantaged workers (Hanson & Johnston, 1985; Madden, 1981).

## 2.4. Conclusion

The past 40 years have seen the implementation, albeit relatively small scale, of dispersal strategies that encourage the relocation of the poor to the suburbs, through the construction of affordable housing or provision of vouchers, and mobility programs that help the disadvantaged connect to suburban job opportunities. These attempts to achieve a more just distribution of the population throughout the region, connecting the poor to housing and jobs, have largely failed to meet even their own goals. Even if they do not work, they remain hotly debated (Briggs, 2008; Imbroscio, 2008). Busy attacking or defending dispersal and mobility policies, neither side is asking a key question: what would a just alternative look like?

## 3. Key concepts of justice underlying the idea of regional accessibility

The argument that we should create an even landscape of opportunity through strategies that change the spatial distribution of the population finds much of its moral underpinnings in the work of John Rawls (1971). Although references to Rawls are not explicit in the literature, and policy-makers do not consciously use liberal theories of justice to address the uneven geography of opportunity, Rawls' work provides a useful framework to understand the characteristic beliefs, rooted in the twentieth-century liberal project, that undergird the policy solutions advocated (O'Connor, 2001). There are three components of Rawls' theory of justice that are relevant to the regional accessibility argument: the "difference principle," the idea of "primary goods," and the "original position."

## 3.1. The difference principle

In his second principle of justice (the difference principle), Rawls argues that:

> Social and economic inequalities are to be arranged so that they are both (a) to the greatest expected benefit of the least advantaged and (b) attached to offices and positions open to all under conditions of fair equality of opportunity. (1971, p. 72)

The idea of equality of opportunity is not just that "offices and positions" are open to all, but that all have the opportunity to acquire the skills necessary in order to achieve in a meritocracy. Rawls acknowledges that social and economic inequality is pervasive and does not suggest that the distribution of wealth and income should be equal, but that it should be to everyone's advantage. In remedying inequalities, maintaining some unequal distribution is justifiable as long as it is to the benefit of all. In order to be just, the more fortunate can benefit disproportionately so long as the condition of the least well-off improves relative to their previous state.

As in Rawls, the argument for dispersal and mobility starts from the position that the distribution of opportunities and resources across metropolitan areas is unjust. As has been well documented elsewhere (for example, Dreier, Mollenkopf, & Swanstrom, 2005), economic restructuring reinforced by public policy exacerbated existing inequalities within metropolitan areas by the end of the twentieth century, with increasing concentrations of poverty in the inner city and affluence in the suburbs. Equity regionalists focusing on regional accessibility seek to establish a more just distribution by breaking up pockets of poverty, creating more housing choice in the suburbs, and revitalizing the old inner-city neighborhoods with an influx of upper-income residents. For instance, Briggs (2004, pp. 329–331) argues for pursuing strategies that "cure" segregation (through changing where people live) rather than mitigate its effects (through improving services), because "expanding housing choice is a linchpin for any agenda to ensure equal opportunity." Regionalists are not so naïve as to think this will fully remedy inequality, but they do expect the change to improve the condition of the least well-off by putting them in an environment rich with resources and opportunities; at a minimum, fair governance coupled with less isolation from the mainstream should level the playing field. If opportunity depends on the ability of individuals to acquire skills to succeed in the meritocracy, then living in the suburbs is key.

Has equity regionalism succeeded in providing more equality of opportunity, with the least advantaged all experiencing some improvement? The overview of regional accessibility strategies, above, suggests a mixed, but mostly failed record. The impact of the new wave of dispersal and mobility policies on equality of opportunity is questionable. Political constraints have prevented fair share housing programs from achieving their promise. In the best case (the MTO program, rather than HOPE VI), dispersal policies have helped families to move to residential neighborhoods with lower levels of poverty. But even so, direct benefits to the families are limited. Families feel safer and they report some inconsistent improvements in mental health. But there are conspicuously no benefits in employment, income, welfare dependency, or physical health. Further, many of the families suffer significant interruptions in their social networking. Likewise, mobility programs, particularly reverse commuting programs, have failed to improve access to jobs and thus do not have an impact on equality of opportunity. In other words, dispersal and mobility policies are failing even to meet the Rawlsian condition of benefit to all, since life-chances are not improving in the new neighborhoods relative to the former neighborhoods.

Justifiable from the Rawlsian perspective is the fact that the well-off may benefit even more than the disadvantaged. Whether or not the intent of policy-makers, dispersal policy offers significant – even disproportionate – benefits to the affluent. In particular, HOPE VI, which has replaced low-income housing with moderate-income and market-rate housing in the urban core, has helped more affluent residents not only move near downtown, but recapture land value in choice neighborhoods nearby.

## 3.2. *Primary goods*

In order to realize opportunity, individuals need equality in "primary goods." These are defined as the prerequisites, both social and natural, for rational individuals to achieve their life-plans. Social goods include rights, liberties, and opportunities, which confer the capacity to realize goals, but also income and wealth. Natural goods include health, intelligence, and imagination. According to Rawls, these add up to self-respect: a sense of one's own value and confidence in one's ability to carry out one's life-plan.

From the equity regionalist perspective, the suburbs offer more equality in primary goods than cities do. The suburbs not only improve access to opportunity but also offer a higher quality of life (Dreier et al., 2005). In the city, the persistent and unsafe ghetto culture, also known as the culture of poverty, reflects the lack of self-respect and devaluing of human life, particularly among low-income minorities (Wilson 1987, 1996). But in the suburbs, the quality of public services and schools is better, neighborhoods are safer and friendlier, and the sense of community is greater. By implication, ghetto culture will not take hold in the suburbs and thus will not hinder the acquisition of primary goods there.

This assumes, of course, that the suburbs do offer enhanced opportunities to acquire skills: that suburban schools are of high quality, jobs are plentiful and accessible, and social systems and networks are inclusive. In practice, however, the failure of dispersal and mobility programs challenges this assumption. Although the new neighborhoods may offer relatively more primary goods, this masks the fact that the families are by and large relocating to other high-poverty, racially segregated neighborhoods. And often, the suburbs do not improve primary goods. For instance, relocatees typically experience difficulty rebuilding social networks, and perhaps because of this are unable to improve in terms of economic opportunity. Likewise, they do not experience improved health outcomes, perhaps because of losing access to health services and institutions once located outside the urban core. Finally, in the case of mobility programs, such as the Bridges to Work program, reverse commuters may actually end up in weaker labor markets than in the central city.

Researchers and policy-makers are aware, of course, that the suburbs no longer provide the opportunities and amenities they once did (Lucy & Phillips, 2000; Orfield, 2002). But they argue that accessing primary goods is simply a matter of moving the disadvantaged further out, beyond the "containment" of the urban core and at-risk inner-ring suburbs (Briggs, 2004, p. 8). In other words, the solution remains spatial, not structural.

*3.3. The original position*

Another component of Rawls' argument that is relevant to the equity regionalist standpoint is the "original position," the idea that everyone should decide principles of justice from behind a "veil of ignorance," a lack of knowledge about their own position in society. In order to further justice, individuals should devise strategies without knowing how she/he will benefit. If we start from this original position, we will maximize the benefit to the least well-off. In other words, the pursuit of justice should be ahistorical.

The regional accessibility argument blames the failed policies of the past, in particular the construction of public housing through the 1950s, the community economic development policies of the 1960s and 1970s, and government-led suburbanization, for regional inequity. Instead, it proposes a set of new policies to even out resources and opportunities across the region. Interestingly, these policies do not build from an understanding of why past policies have failed (e.g. the lack of funding to cover public housing maintenance, the lack of funding for the War on Poverty, and the inability of municipalities to zone for and fund affordable housing) to address these structural issues. Rather, they in essence start from behind the "veil of ignorance": they propose as a solution altogether different governance structures, for instance creating new metropolitan institutions (Dreier et al., 2005).

Further, it is hard to argue that these policies, particularly dispersal, are constructed without stakeholders knowing how they will benefit. For instance, there is clear benefit to the inner-city growth machine in removing low-income residents – yet there is no critical examination of such benefit.

## 4. Dispersal, mobility, and alternative conceptions of justice

The ideas of equality of opportunity and choice underlie much of equity regionalist policy, even if it has had little success at these goals. The psychological literature on values and economic class helps explain why pursuing equality of opportunity alone may not be the most just approach. Critics of urban renewal have shown how the experience of relocation can be traumatic for low-income residents (Fried, 1966; Fullilove, 2004). More recent surveys on economic insecurity have demonstrated that people strongly prefer stability to opportunity, given a choice between the *status quo* and uncertain future earnings (Hacker, 2008). The lower the income, the more choice is associated with fear, doubt, and difficulty: "While the upper and middle classes define freedom as choice, working-class Americans emphasize freedom from instability" (Schwartz, Markus, & Snibbe, 2006, p. 15).

There are other ways to frame the issues of justice and opportunity in the inner city. The capabilities approach (Nussbaum, 2000; Sen, 1999) shifts our focus to what inner-city residents are able to do or be, instead of how much they can achieve in purely economic terms. Related to this is the idea that needs differ among groups, so the Rawlsian set of primary goods may not apply uniformly to all and equal starting points may not mean equal outcomes (Fainstein, 2006; Harvey, 1973; Nussbaum, 2000). Another line of argument lies in the concept of a "right to the city" (Lefebvre, 1996), which includes the right to urban life and its centrality, vitality, and visibility (Fainstein, 2006; Mitchell, 2003).

## *4.1. Capabilities*

The capabilities approach (Sen, 1999) suggests that instead of thinking about distribution in terms of the resources people are able to access, we should examine what their environmental context allows them to do or be. Capabilities encompass many of Rawls' social and natural goods, but also include the pursuit of "affiliation":

> being able to live with and toward others, to recognize and show concern for other human beings, to engage in various forms of social interaction; to be able to imagine the situation of another and to have compassion for that situation; to have the capability for both justice and friendship. (Nussbaum, 2000, p. 79)

The idea of affiliation acknowledges the use value of urban space, which Lefebvre incorporates into his idea of city as "oeuvre," or a collective project in which all of its citizens participate. The tension between use value and exchange value fosters battles for urban land: "This city is itself 'oeuvre', a feature which contrasts with the irreversible tendency towards money and commerce, towards exchange and products. Indeed the oeuvre is use value and the product is exchange value" (Lefebvre, 1996, p. 66). Residents have a right to the oeuvre, since it allows them to meet their social needs, which:

> include the need for security and opening, the need for certainty and adventure, that of organization of work and of play, the needs or the predictable and the unpredictable, of similarity and difference, of isolation and encounter, exchange and investments, of independence (even solitude) and communication, of immediate and long-term prospects. (Lefebvre, 1996, p. 147)

As Fainstein (2006) and other critics point out, the Rawlsian focus on equality among individuals sidesteps these issues of social affiliation and needs. Omitting the collectivity from the discussion means that certain types of goods – particularly those associated with social affiliation – are not considered important: "The starting point of individual liberty also avoids questions that bear on the character of collective goods – e.g. a high-quality built environment – if they are not necessary for the development of capabilities or remedying inequality" (Fainstein, 2006, p. 17).

Thus, it is perhaps not surprising that some equity regionalist strategies – in particular, dispersal and mobility strategies – have met with mixed success. If dispersal has not improved access to natural goods, such as health, and social goods, such as economic opportunity, then the move to the suburbs may actually hinder the development of capabilities. If the development of capabilities rests in part on meeting the need for social affiliation, then the disruption of social networks that occurs when the spatial distribution of the population changes may likewise affect capabilities negatively.

The concept of the "oeuvre" sheds light on why mobility strategies have not succeeded in helping city residents access suburban jobs. Strategies that purely promote physical access to jobs ignore the intricate social system through which people find jobs – let alone the workforce development system, which, at its best, provides a valuable channel for information about the labor market (Chapple, 2006).

What would an urban poverty policy that supported the need for affiliation look like? If the goal of US anti-poverty policy remains breaking up concentrations of poverty, there are alternatives to vouchering out residents to the suburbs. First, the government could offer the option of staying in decent housing in the neighborhood (but outside the blocks with very high-poverty population). This would entail purchasing or securing below-market-rate units in the vicinity and making them permanently affordable. In the case of urban renewal projects, this replacement housing should be ready before demolition commences. Second, the government could provide income or work supports (from an enhanced Earned Income Tax Credit to childcare and transportation assistance) to working poor residents so that they could better afford market-rate units in the city. Third, cities could leverage existing programs, such as their inclusionary zoning requirements, to house residents from concentrated poverty areas.

## 4.2. *Differing needs*

We turn next to the issue of whether and how needs for primary goods differ among groups. From a Rawlsian perspective on how to create equality of opportunity, policy-makers would first need to measure how residents of concentrated poverty neighborhoods are faring in terms of resources. This apparently assumes a homogeneous public with similar levels of needs (Young, 1990). Yet, as Harvey (1973) points out, different groups have different elasticities in use of resources, so equality of opportunity depends on social context. For instance, if people lack "cultural motivation" to use parks, developing such facilities for them will not lead to a more just income distribution (Harvey, 1973). Housing opportunity is another of Harvey's examples (also see Gans, 1968): "Low-income groups, for example often identify very closely with their housing environment and the psychological cost of moving is to them far greater than it is to the mobile upper middle class" (Harvey, 1973, p. 85).

Suppose that metropolitan areas were reorganized so that each individual had the same level of resources and opportunities, or at least a threshold level: social services, amenities, education and work opportunities are distributed equally across the region, in a utopian spatial allocation. Yet, utility differs: "giving resources to people does not always bring differently situated people up to the same level of capability to function" (Nussbaum, 2000, p. 99). Coming from different backgrounds, some may lack the ability to use resources in order to function better. In fact, Nussbaum (2000, p. 69) argues that assuming resources benefit all equally "doesn't sufficiently respect the struggle of each and every individual for flourishing."

In a context of differing needs, a metropolitan landscape of equal opportunity may mean little. Housing choice vouchers will disproportionately benefit those with the mobility to assess housing opportunity throughout a region, as well as those without special housing needs – and will not necessarily meet the needs of those who are attached to their neighborhood and do not wish to move. Having jobs in close proximity means little without the network resources to get hired (Chapple, 2006).

In contrast, the capabilities approach looks at what it would actually take to realize a life-plan, which may entail more resources, social supports, and/or other assistance. An anti-poverty policy that supported capabilities would need to understand differences in utility among different population sub-groups. Although ideally this would entail conducting detailed assessments prior to implementing new housing policies, this approach may not be practical. Instead, it might be possible to use existing knowledge about needs to guide intervention. For instance, since studies have repeatedly found that lower-income groups value stability and security more than freedom of choice, it would be important to offer the urban disadvantaged stable and central housing options in addition to opportunities to relocate throughout the metropolitan area.

### 4.3. *The right to the city*

Another approach to social justice is the "right to the city" (Lefebvre, 1996), which encompasses the ideas of diversity, amenity, and visibility. Fostering diversity is key to justice because it helps us imagine alternative futures and life-plans. The city makes possible encounters with people who are different, which in turn enriches experience. Thus the just city "ought to provide spaces in which valuably different forms of human activity can flourish" (Nussbaum, 2000, p. 60).

For the disadvantaged, being seen is just as important as seeing others. For Lefebvre, the right to the city is essentially the right to inhabit, or the right of individuals and groups to shape the conditions of their existence in space. With the right to inhabit, oppressed groups can stay visible in the public eye. Possessing this "space for representation" helps give groups legitimacy in their struggles (Mitchell, 2003, p. 33).

As inner cities revitalize – and as public housing becomes mixed-income development – affluent newcomers squeeze out the disadvantaged. This threatens urban diversity and even the visibility of the least well-off. It also suggests another right: the right to enjoy "renewed centrality" (Lefebvre, 1996, p. 179): "The right to the city ought to refer to more than mere inclusion – it needs to encompass access to an appealing city" (Fainstein, 2006, p. 18).

The spatial solution offered by dispersal and mobility strategies conflicts directly with the right to the city. Vouchered out of downtown public housing, the poor lose their centrality, visibility, and access to diversity. Commuting out to jobs in the suburbs, jobseekers lose their connections to the urban economy. Urban anti-poverty policy should prioritize stable affordable housing in central locations, and use overall job accessibility as a criterion to identify appropriate replacement housing. Indeed, planners have a growing toolkit to create more equitable development in the face of gentrification, including community land trusts, just cause eviction controls, employer-assisted housing, and other policies (PolicyLink, 2004).

### 5. Conclusion: does equity regionalism create a just metro?

In the aftermath of Hurricane Katrina, some 160 academics, led by Xavier de Souza Briggs and William Julius Wilson, suggested in a petition to Congress that there would be a silver lining as New Orleans residents would be able to "move to opportunity." In stinging rebuttals, critics argued that policy-makers and researchers supporting dispersal policies are imposing their own values and norms on the poor, and aim to make poverty invisible rather than address its causes (Imbroscio, 2008; Reed & Steinberg, 2006). By two years later, research had shown that the relocatees were faring worse than those who returned to New Orleans, regardless of whether they had moved to a stronger regional economy (Vigdor, 2007). Perhaps opportunity is not enough to solve poverty.

Casting justice in terms of equality of opportunity alone means neglecting the non-economic aspects of life – capabilities, social needs, urban life and vitality. The dispersal and mobility policy alternatives show little concern for these needs. Changing the spatial distribution of the population may create a more optimal and equitable spatial allocation, but in some ways it fails to acknowledge basic human aspirations to live in security, in community, or in a revitalized core. In the case of regionalist dispersal programs, the attempt to achieve greater equality has even destroyed human dignity, in an uncanny replay of the urban renewal era (Goetz, 2003). It is not that opportunity does not matter, but rather that these spatial fixes are dually flawed: they fail to acknowledge the strengths of urban life, and they deflect attention from the real problem, lack of federal initiatives and funding to address issues of poverty, inequality, and insecurity.

How is it that discussion of these policies continues, despite their shortcomings in addressing social equity? Arguably, they help build coalitions between the left and the right. Policies from dispersal to tax base sharing allow leftists to blame place rather than individuals – yet without blaming capitalism itself. Thus the left (as led by Loic Wacquant) remains enamored of the idea of an advanced marginality embedded in space, despite the rising deconcentration of the poor and their new exploitation in the era of Wal-Martization (Marcuse, 2007; Wacquant, 2007). On the right, regionalist approaches gain support because they shift our gaze away from the defunding of anti-poverty and public housing programs, offering a set of solutions with low government cost (many of which also increase property values).

In some arenas, a new bottom-up or multi-level equity regionalism is upending these old top-down approaches. Although not explicitly inspired by alternative conceptions of justice, many are advocating approaches that build on basic human aspirations and needs, rather than get implemented in spite of them because of an undue focus on ends rather than means. A regional equity movement, or "social movement regionalism," is building coalitions for economic justice, with considerable success in mobilizing constituencies at a regional scale for causes from living wages to community benefits (Pastor, Benner, & Matsuoka, 2009). Also emerging are informal regional governance strategies employed by networks of public, private, and civic actors. In particular, community-based organizations are using networks to exert power at the regional, state, and federal levels, in a process of multi-level governance (Swanstrom & Banks, 2008; Weir & Rongerude, 2007). Finally, a string of community economic development successes has led some (for example, Alperovitz, Williamson, & Imbroscio, 2002) to argue that Rusk (1999) and others proclaimed the death of the inside game too soon. Although the "poor in a loomp" may well be bad, we may finally be learning that using a spatial fix to destroy or move the loomp is not the solution.

**References**

Alperovitz, G., Williamson, T., & Imbroscio, D. (2002). Community land trusts and community agriculture. In *Making a place for community: Local democracy in a global era* (pp. 249–264). New York: Routledge Press.

Altshuler, A., et al. (1999). *Governance and opportunity in metropolitan America*. Washington, DC: National Academy Press.

Bair, E., & Fitzgerald, J.M. (2005). Hedonic estimation and policy significance of the impact of HOPE VI on neighborhood property values. *Review of Policy Research, 22*(6), 771–786.

Barrett, E.J., Geisel, P., & Johnston, J. (2006). *The Ramoni Utti report: Impacts of the Ripley Arnold relocation program*. Prepared for the City of Fort Worth, Texas. School of Urban and Public Affairs, University of Texas at Arlington.

Basolo, V., & Hastings, D. (2003). Obstacles to regional housing solutions: A comparison of four metropolitan areas. *Journal of Urban Affairs, 25*(4), 449–472.

Bollens, S. (2003). In through the back door: Social equity and regional governance. *Housing Policy Debate, 13*(4), 631–657.

Brenner, N. (2002). Decoding the newest "metropolitan regionalism" in the USA: A critical overview. *Cities, 19*(1), 3–21.

Briggs, X. (1998). Brown kids in white suburbs: Housing mobility and the many faces of social capital. *Housing Policy Debate, 9*(1), 177–221.

Briggs, X. (Ed.). (2004). *The geography of opportunity: Race and housing choice in metropolitan America*. Washington, DC: Brookings Institution Press.

Briggs, X. (2008). Maximum feasible misdirection: A reply to Imbroscio. *Journal of Urban Affairs, 30*(2), 131–137.

Brooks, F., Zugazaga, C., Wolk, J., & Adams, M.A. (2005). Resident perceptions of housing, neighborhood, and economic conditions after relocation from public housing undergoing HOPE VI redevelopment. *Research on Social Work Practice, 15*(6), 481–490.

Buron, L., Levy, D.K., & Gallagher, M. (2007). *Housing choice vouchers: How HOPE VI families fared in the private market* (Urban Institute Policy Brief No. 3). Washington, DC: The Urban Institute.

Buron, L., Popkin, S., Levy, D., Harris, L., & Khadduri, J. (2002). *The HOPE VI resident tracking study: A snapshot of the current living situation of original residents from eight sites*. Washington, DC: The Urban Institute.

Calavita, N., Grimes, K., & Mallach, N. (1997). Inclusionary housing in California and New Jersey: A comparative analysis. *Housing Policy Debate, 8*(1), 109–142.

Campbell, H. (2006). Just planning: The art of situated ethical judgment. *Journal of Planning Education and Research, 26*(1), 92–106.

Chapple, K. (2006). Overcoming mismatch: Beyond dispersal, mobility, and development strategies. *Journal of the American Planning Association, 72*(3), 322–336.

Clampet-Lundquist, S. (2004). Moving over or moving up? Short-term gains and losses for relocated HOPE VI families. *Cityscape, 7*(1), 57–80.

Clampet-Lundquist, S. (2007). No more 'Bois ball: The impact of relocation from public housing on adolescents. *Journal of Adolescent Research, 22*(3), 298–323.

Clampet-Lundquist, S., Edin, K., Kling, J.R., & Duncan, G.J. (2006)*Moving at-risk teenagers out of high-risk neighborhoods: Why girls fare better than boys* (Princeton IRS Working Paper 509). Princeton, NJ: Princeton University.

Comey, J. (2007) *HOPE VI'd and on the move* (Urban Institute Policy Brief No. 1, June). Washington, DC: The Urban Institute.

Crain, R.L. (1970). School integration and occupational achievement of negroes. *American Journal of Sociology, 75*(4), 593–606.

Curley, A. (2006). *HOPE and housing: The effects of relocation on movers' economic stability, social networks, and health*. Unpublished dissertation, Boston University.

Dreier, P., Mollenkopf, J., & Swanstrom, T. (2005). *Place matters: Metropolitics for the twety-first century* (2nd ed.). Lawrence: University Press of Kansas.

Fainstein, S. (2006). *Planning and the just city*. Unpublished paper presented at Searching for the Just City Conference, Columbia University, New York City.

Fried, M. (1966). Grieving for a lost home. In James Q. Wilson (Ed.), *Urban renewal: The record and the controversy* (pp. 359–379). Cambridge, MA: MIT Press.

Fullilove, M.T. (2004). *Root shock: How tearing up city neighborhoods hurt America and what we can do about it*. New York: Ballantine Books.

Gallagher, M., & Bajaj, B. (2007). *Moving on: Benefits and challenges of HOPE VI for children* (Urban Institute Policy Brief No. 4, June). Washington, DC: The Urban Institute.

Galster, G. & Killen, S. (1995). Geography of metropolitan opportunity: A reconnaissance and conceptual framework. *Housing Policy Debate, 6*(1), 7–43.

Gans, H. (1968). The failure of urban renewal: A critique and some proposals. In *People and plans: Essays on urban problems and solutions* (pp. 260–277). New York: Basic Books.

Gibson, K. (2007)The relocation of the Columbia Villa community: Views from Residents. *Journal of Planning Education and Research, 27*(1), 5–19.

Goering, J., & Feins, J.D. (2003). *Choosing a better life: Evaluating the moving to opportunity social experiment*. Washington, DC: Urban Institute Press.

Goetz, E.G. (2002). Forced relocation vs. voluntary mobility: The effects of dispersal programs on households. *Housing Studies, 17*(1), 107–123.

Goetz, E.G. (2003). *Clearing the way: Deconcentrating the poor in urban America*. Washington, DC: Urban Institute Press.

Goetz, E.G., Chapple, K., & Lukermann, B. (2003). Enabling exclusion: The retreat from regional fair share housing in the implementation of the Minnesota Land Use Planning Act. *Journal of Planning Education and Research, 22*(3), 213–225.

Goetz, E.G., & Flack, A.V. (2008). *Regional fair share housing: Estimating need and rewarding performance*. Unpublished manuscript, Humphrey Institute of Public Affairs, Minneapolis, MN.

Greenbaum, S., Hathaway, W., Rodrigez, C., Spalding, A., & Ward, B. (2008). Deconcentration and social capital: Contradictions of a poverty alleviation policy. *Journal of Poverty, 12*(2), 201–228.

Hacker, J.S. (2008). *The great risk shift: The new economic insecurity and the decline of the American dream*. New York: Oxford University Press.

Hanson, S., & Johnston, I. (1985). Gender differences in work-trip lengths: Explanations and implications. *Urban Geography, 6*, 193–219.

Harvey, D. (1973). *Social justice and the city*. Baltimore, MD: The Johns Hopkins Press.

Hughes, M.A. (1995). A mobility strategy for improving opportunity. *Housing Policy Debate, 6*, 271–297.

Imbroscio, D. (2006). Shaming the inside game: A critique of the liberal expansionist approach to addressing urban problems. *Urban Affairs Review, 42*(2), 224–248.

Imbroscio, D. (2008). United and actuated by some common impulse of passion: Challenging the dispersal consensus in American housing policy research. *Journal of Urban Affairs, 30*(2), 111–130.

Kain, J.F. (1992). The spatial mismatch hypothesis: Three decades later. *Housing Policy Debate, 3*(2), 371–460.

Kaufman, J. & Rosenbaum, J. (1992). The education and employment of low-income black youth in white suburbs. *Educational Evaluation and Policy Analysis, 14*, 229–240.

Kleit, R.G., & Manzo, L.C. (2006). To move or not to move: Relationships to place and relocation choices in HOPE VI. *Housing Policy Debate, 17*(2), 271–308.

Kling, J.R., & Liebman, J.B. (2004). *Experimental analysis of neighborhood effects on youth* (Princeton IRS Working Paper No. 483). Princeton, NJ: Princeton University.

Kling, J.R., Liebman, J.B., & Katz, L.F. (2007). Experimental analysis of neighborhood effects on youth. *Econometrica, Econometric Society, 75*(1), 83–119.

Lefebvre, H. (1996). *Writings on Cities* (E. Kofman and E. Lebas, Ed. and Trans.). Cambridge, MA: Blackwell.

Levy, D.K., & Woolley, M. (2007). *Relocation is not enough: Employment barriers among HOPE VI families* (Urban Institute Policy Brief No. 6). Washington, DC: The Urban Institute.

Listokin, D. (1976). *Fair share housing allocation*. New Brunswick: Center for Urban Policy Research.

Lucy, W., & D. Phillips. (2000). *Confronting suburban decline: Strategic planning for metropolitan renewal*. Washington, DC: Island Press.

Lund, B. (1999). "The poor in a loomp is bad": New labour and neighborhood renewal. *Political Quarterly, 70*(3), 280–284.

Madden, J. (1981). Why women work closer to home. *Urban Studies, 18*, 181–194.

Manjarrez, C.A., Popkin, S.J., & Guernsey, E. (2007). *Poor health: Adding insult to injury for HOPE VI families* (Urban Institute Policy Brief No. 5).

Marcuse, P. (2007). Putting space in its place: Reassessing the spatiality of the ghetto and advanced marginality. *City, 11*(3), 378–383.

Mitchell, D. (2003). *The right to the city: Social justice and the fight for public space.* New York: Guilford Press.

Nussbaum, M. (2000). *Women and human development: The capabilities approach.* New York: Cambridge University Press.

O'Connor, A. (2001). *Poverty knowledge: Social science, social policy, and the poor in twentieth-century U.S. history.* Princeton, NJ: Princeton University Press.

O'Regan, K.M., & Quigley, J.M. (1999). *Spatial isolation and welfare recipients: What do we know? Berkeley Program on Housing and Urban Policy* (Working Paper W99-003). Berkeley, CA: University of California, Berkeley.

Orfield, M. (1997). *Metropolitics: A regional agenda for community and stability.* Washington, DC: Brookings Institution Press.

Orfield, M. (2002). *American metropolitics: A comparative national study of social separation and sprawl.* Washington, DC: Brookings Institution.

Pastor, M., Benner, C., & Matsuoka, M. (2009). *This could be the start of something big: Regional equity organizing and the future of metropolitan America.* Ithaca, NY: Cornell University Press.

PolicyLink. (2004). *Equitable development toolkit.* Oakland, CA: PolicyLink. Retrieved February 14, 2008, from http://www.policylink.org/EDTK/

Popkin, S.J. (2006). The HOPE VI program: What has happened to the residents? In L.Bennett, J.L.Smith, & P.A.Wright (Eds.), *Where are poor people to live: Transforming public housing communities (cities and contemporary society)* (pp. 68–90). Armonk, NY: M.E. Sharpe.

Popkin, S.J., & Cove, E. (2007). *Safety is the most important thing: How HOPE VI helped families* (Urban Institute Policy Brief No. 2). Washington, DC: The Urban Institute.

Popkin, S.J., Katz, B., Cunningham, M.K., Brown, K., Gustafson, J., & Turner, M.A. (2004). *A decade of Hope VI: Research findings and policy challenges.* Washington, DC: The Urban Institute.

Popkin, S.J., Rosenbaum, J., & Meaden, P. (1993). Labor market experiences of low-income black women in middle-class suburbs. *Journal of Policy Analysis and Management, 12*(3), 556–573.

Putnam, R. (2007). *E pluribus unum*: Diversity and community in the twenty-first century – The 2006 Johan Skytte Prize Lecture. *Scandinavian Political Studies, 30*(2), 137–174.

Rawls, J. (1971). *A theory of justice.* Massaze: Belknap Press of Harvard University Press.

Reed, A., & Steinberg, S. (2006). Liberal bad faith in the wake of Hurricane Katrinca. *Black Commentator, 182.* Retrieved from www.blackcommentator.com/182/182_cover_liberals_katrina_pf.html

Roder, A., & Scrivner, S. (2005). *Seeking a sustainable journey to work: Findings from the National Bridges to Work Demonstration.* Philadelphia: Public/Private Ventures.

Rosenbaum, J.E., & Popkin, S.J. (1991). Employment and earnings of low-income blacks who move to middle-class suburbs. In *The urban underclass* (pp. 342–356). Washington, DC: The Brookings Institute.

Rosenbloom, S. (1992). *Reverse commute transportation: emerging provide roles.* Washington, DC: Urban Mass Transportation Administration, US Department of Transportation.

Rubinowitz, L.S., & Rosenbaum, J.E. (2000). *Crossing the class and color lines: From public housing to white suburbia.* Chicago: University of Chicago Press.

Rusk, D. (1999). *Inside game/outside game: Winning strategies for saving urban America.* Washington, DC: Brookings Institution Press.

Sanbonmatsu, L., Kling, J.R., Duncan,G.R., & Brooks-Gunn, J. (2006). Neighborhoods and academic achievement: Results from the Moving To Opportunity experiment. *Journal of Human Resources, 41*(4), 649–691.

Schwartz, B., Markus, H.R., & Snibbe, A.C. (2006). *Is freedom just another word for many things to buy?* New York: New York Times

Sen, A. (1999). *Development as freedom.* New York: Anchor.

Swanstrom, T. & Banks, B. (2009). Going regional: Community-based regionalism, transportation, and local hiring agreements. *Journal of Planning Education and Research, 28*, 355–367.

Turney, K., Clampet-Lundquist, S., Edin, K., Kling, J.R., & Duncan G.J. (2006). *Neighborhood effects on barriers to employment: Results from a randomized housing mobility experiment in Baltimore* (IRS Working Paper 511). Princeton: Princeton University.

Vigdor, J.L. (2007). The Katrina effect: Was there a bright side to the evacuation of Greater New Orleans? *The B.E. Journal of Economic Analysis & Policy, 7*, 1–38.

Wacquant, L. (2007). *Urban outcasts: A Comparative sociology of advanced marginality.* Cambridge, UK: Polity.

Weir, M. & Rongerude, J. (2007). *Multi-Level power and progressive regionalism.* Institute of Governmental Studies Working Paper 2007–15. Berkeley, CA: University of California, Berkeley.

Wexler, H.J. (2001). HOPE VI: Market means/public ends – the goals, strategies, and midterm lessons of HUD's Urban Revitalization Demonstration Program. *Journal of Affordable Housing, 10*(3), 195–233.

Wilson, W.J. (1987). *The truly disadvantaged: The inner city, the underclass, and public policy.* Chicago: The University of Chicago Press.

Wilson, W.J. (1996). *When work disappears.* New York: Vintage.

Wish, N.B., & Eisdorfer, S. (1997). The impact of mount laurel initiatves: An analysis of the characteristics of applicants and occupants. *Seton Hall Law Review, 27*, 1268–1337.

Young, I.M. (1990). *Justice and the politics of difference.* Princeton, NJ: Princeton University Press.

Zielenbach, S. (2003). Assessing economic change in HOPE VI neighborhoods. *Housing Policy Debate, 14*(4), 621–655.

# The role of community-based strategies in addressing metropolitan segregation and racial health disparities

Malo André Hutson[a] and Sacoby Wilson[b]

[a]Department of City and Regional Planning, University of California at Berkeley, Berkeley, CA, USA; [b]Institute for Families in Society, Department of Epidemiology and Biostatistics, University of South Carolina, Columbia, SC, USA

> This paper is a conceptual analysis of the effects of racial residential segregation, which is a major contributor to racial and ethnic health disparities. Metropolitan segregation has had adverse health consequences for economically disadvantaged and minority populations because they are exposed to higher levels of environmental pollutants and have limited opportunities to gain a quality education, access to healthcare, and increase their economic opportunity. Based on our empirical and theoretical analysis we provide a holistic framework that takes an ecological systems approach to understand the affects of urban health and health disparities. We contend that in order to improve the urban/environmental health conditions for the most vulnerable urban populations, it will require comprehensive community and regional focused strategies that link local community development efforts to larger macro-level metropolitan regional strategies.

## Metropolitan segregation and health disparities

Where a person lives and grows up can have a significant impact on their life-chances and quality of life. This is especially the case within the United States where the health status of an individual or group of individuals can vary widely depending on the block, neighborhood, or metropolitan area in which they reside (Fitzpatrick & LaGory, 2000). In the US federal, state, and local policies along with institutionalized racism have contributed to inequitable development across metropolitan areas, resulting in widening racial/ethnic and class divisions and unequal social and economic opportunities for economically disadvantaged residents (Dreier, Mollenkopf, & Swanstrom, 2004; Frug, 1999; Lopez, 2004; Williams & Collins, 2001). Moreover, inequitable metropolitan development results in the concentration of unhealthy living conditions and environments, which contributes to racial and ethnic health disparities.

According to the latest National Center for Health Statistion mortality data, racial and ethnic health disparities between blacks and whites and Hispanics and whites are significant (see Table 1).

Table 1. Age-adjusted death rates by for black, Hispanic and white ratios for the 10 leading causes of death, United States 2007.

| Rank | Causes | Black to white ratio | Hispanic to white ratio |
|---|---|---|---|
|  | All causes | 1.3 | 0.7 |
| 1 | Heart disease | 1.3 | 0.7 |
| 2 | Cancer | 1.2 | 0.6 |
| 3 | Stroke | 1.5 | 0.8 |
| 4 | Pulmonary disease | 0.7 | 0.4 |
| 5 | Accidents | 0.9 | 0.7 |
| 6 | Alzheimer's disease | 0.8 | 0.6 |
| 7 | Diabetes | 2.1 | 1.5 |
| 8 | Flu and pneumonia | 1.2 | 0.8 |
| 9 | Kidney disease | 2.2 | 0.9 |
| 10 | Blood poisoning | 2.2 | 0.8 |

Note: Taken from Centers for Disease Control (2010).

Blacks have an overall mortality rate that is 1.3 times that of whites and Hispanics have a lower overall mortality rate than whites at 0.7. In analyzing the top 10 leading causes of death for 2007, the disparity in mortality ratio between blacks and whites was the highest for kidney disease (2.2) and blood poisoning (2.2), followed by diabetes (2.1), and stroke (1.5). Hispanics had a higher mortality ratio between whites only for diabetes (1.5). Although it appears that Hispanics have overall lower mortality ratios compared with whites it is worth noting that this could be for several reasons. According to David Williams and others, a high number of non-black minorities are classified as white on the death certificate, which leads to an underestimate of the death rates for Hispanics (Hahn, 1992; Sorlie, Rogot, & Johnson, 1993; Williams, 1999). In addition, a high proportion of Hispanics are foreign-born, thus reflecting the fact that immigrants tend to have better health status than the native-born population (Hummer, Rogers, Nam, & LeClere, 1999; Singh & Yu, 1996; Williams, 1999).

Perhaps one of the biggest factors contributing to differences in racial and ethnic health disparities has been residential segregation (Acevedo-Garcia, Osypuk, McArdle, & Williams, 2008; Corburn, 2009; Massey, 2004; Williams & Collins, 2001). Racial residential segregation directly impacts ethnic minorities' socio-economic status (SES) at the individual, household, and community levels, which can negatively influence their health status (Ahmed, Mohammed, & Williams, 2007; Corburn, 2009; Massey & Denton, 1993; Williams & Collins, 2001). Lower socioeconomic and racially segregated minority communities and neighborhoods tend to have limited access to necessities such as quality housing, education, medical care, healthy foods, and economic opportunities – all of which are important determinants of health, especially economic opportunities. Sociologist William Julius Wilson describes the effects of deindustrialization and racial residential segregation on the economic opportunities for blacks in Chicago. He argues that highly concentrated urban poor communities "offer few legitimate employment opportunities, inadequate job information networks, and poor schools," all of which lead to the disappearance of work (Wilson, 1996, p. 52).

In addition to limited employment opportunities, poorer racially segregated communities within urban metropolitan communities offer less access to a broad range of services provided by municipal governments (Alba & Logan, 1993; Hutson, Kaplan, Ranjit, & Mujahid, 2011; Williams, 1999). A recent study that analyzed the largest 171 metropolitan areas within the United States according to metropolitan jurisdictional fragmentation and racial segregation found that metropolitan areas that were highly fragmented based on the number of governmental jurisdictions had higher overall black white mortality ratios compared with metropolitan areas with less jurisdictional fragmentation (Hutson et al., 2011).

Residential segregation also limits minorities' access to medical care and exposes them to neighborhood environments with higher levels of social disorder, violence and environmental toxins, all of which influence health (Ahmed et al., 2007; LaVeist, 1993; Massey, 2004; Morello-Frosch & Lopez, 2006; Williams, 1999; Williams & Jackson, 2005). In terms of access to medical care, the Institute of Medicine (2002) report *Unequal Treatment: Confronting Racial and Ethnic Disparities in Healthcare* found that some evidence suggests that bias, prejudice, and stereotyping on the part of healthcare providers may contribute to differences in care (2002, p. 195). Lower SES also contributes to lower levels of health insurance for poor, minority residents, resulting in fewer visits to the doctor and less access to preventive medicine (Williams & Jackson, 2005).

Highly racially segregated neighborhoods also tend to have higher exposures to environmental toxins and industrial land uses. For example, within New York City, Julie Sze argues that the most manufacturing zone increases over the years have occurred in the Bronx, an area with the highest concentration of poor and minority residents while Manhattan has experienced the greatest decreases in manufacturing zoning (Sze, 2007). Sze argues that the high level of zoned land for manufacturing within the Bronx exposed its residents to a disproportionate amount of environmental toxins compared with other communities within New York City. The Bronx, like many other poor communities of color, are exposed to unhealthy land uses and industrial production that over time can have an adverse impact on their quality of life and the overall health (Massey, 2004; Morello-Frosch & Lopez, 2006).

It is clear that racial residential segregation indirectly impacts individuals' SES, resulting in a number of deleterious influences that impacts the health status of poor, minority individuals. This raises very important questions. What can be done to address the current racial and ethnic health disparities gap that exists in the United States? What community-based strategies are most effective in addressing metropolitan segregation and racial health disparities?

**Conceptual framework to address community development issues and health disparities**

We should employ a comprehensive framework that considers ecologic features of the built and social environment to enhance community development in unserved and underserved communities hurt by health disparities. This framework (see Figure 1) incorporates elements of community development, urban planning, and the public health perspectives to categorize communities at different levels including neighborhoods, towns, cities, and metropolitan areas as human ecological systems, whereby the overall health of the human ecological system influences health and the degree of health disparities within and between human ecosystems (Wilson, 2009). This approach focuses on understanding how context, place, and local socio-environmental conditions impact the health of populations and individuals (Wilson,

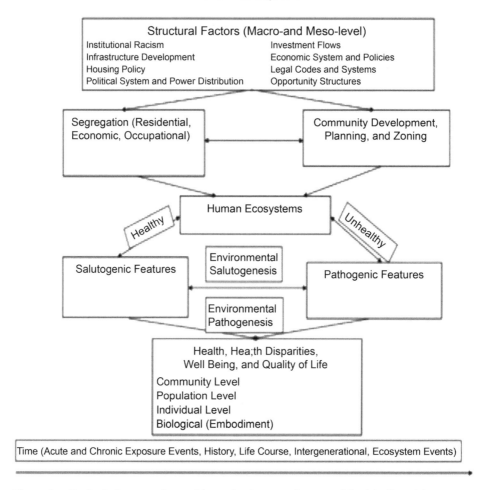

Figure 1. Ecologic framework to address development issues and health disparities.
Note: Figure taken from Wilson (2009).

2009). By modifying the health and quality of our human ecosystems, we can positively impact the lifestyles, health behaviors, health outcomes, and quality of life of populations who reside, work, or play in different ecosystems particularly disadvantaged, historically marginalized, and underserved populations (Wilson, 2009).

The framework builds upon an emerging area of environmental justice research that has explored the contribution of neighborhood stressors, structural factors, neighborhood-level resources, and the built environment to community health and the creation of health disparities (Brulle & Pellow, 2006; Gee & Payne-Sturges, 2004; Morello-Frosch & Lopez, 2006; Payne-Sturges & Gee, 2006; Payne-Sturges, Gee, Crowder, et al., 2006; Soobader, Cubbin, & Gee, 2006; Wilson, 2009), particularly disparities in asthma, adult mortality, infant mortality, cancer, obesity, cardiovascular disease, diabetes, and crime-related health outcomes. Figure 1 shows a conceptual framework that illustrates the role that different fundamental factors and spatial drivers of community context have in how human ecological systems are developed and maintained. The primary structural factors shown in Figure 1, including institutional discrimination and racism, political power, socioeconomic inequality, housing policy, economic systems and development, and investment flows and patterns, operate through and drive spatial processes of segregation and community development (Wilson, 2009). By operating through these spatial processes, these structural factors act as the main determinants of positive and negative health outcomes at the national, regional, metropolitan, neighborhood, population, and individual levels (Wilson, 2009). We can categorize human ecosystems as "healthy" or "unhealthy" based on the number and quality of and access to health-promoting and health-restricting structural (built and social) features measured across physical, social, political, economic, and spiritual spheres (Wilson, 2009).

Spatially uneven and fragmented community and economic development, implementation of housing policies, and opportunity infrastructure have contributed to the production of urban landscapes with a high concentration of locally unwanted land uses (e.g. chemical plants, factories, heavily-trafficked highways, landfills, incinerators, waste treatment facilities, hazardous waste sites), limited number of health-promoting resources, low-quality schools, unemployment, economic instability, urban degradation, crime, violence, and drugs. These unhealthy urban landscapes known as "riskscapes" (Morello-Frosch & Lopez, 2006) or unhealthy urban geographies disparately burden segregated, disadvantaged, and marginalized urban communities (Wilson, 2009). In recent years, urban revitalization and smart growth initiatives have been implemented and supported by community developers, planners, local, state, and federal governments, architects, and non-profit environmental and economic organizations as approaches to improve health and sustainability of urban communities. Unfortunately, many of these initiatives do very little to provide benefits to historically disadvantaged populations (Wilson, 2009). These programs, instead of having positive community benefits for all demographic groups in our cities and towns, may lead to more segregation, gentrification, and community development inequities characteristic of suburbanization and related highway expansion in the mid-1950s and urban renewal later in the 1970s and 1980s (Wilson, 2009).

Fortunately, the new ecosystems approach to human health presented in this paper may allow us to holistically assess, understand, and improve health by using community development to change socioenvironmental conditions. Human ecosystems with negative socioenvironmental conditions can lead to adverse health outcomes, drive bad health behaviors, and result in unhealthy lifestyles for populations within the ecosystems. On the other hand, living in human ecosystems with positive socioenvironmental conditions may lead to good health outcomes, health behaviors, and lifestyles, and improve individual-level, population-level, and community-level quality of life. The integration of the health promotion and prevention approach in community development and planning may catalyze a change in the life-course trajectory of at-risk and vulnerable populations and human ecosystems (Wilson, 2009). Therefore, the use of community development and planning initiatives and environmental health policies that help foster salutogenic (health-promoting) social and built environments may have important implications for public health in human ecosystems, particularly for disadvantaged, underserved, and marginalized populations who are disparately burdened by both environmental (i.e. landfills, incinerators, environmental hazards, air pollution, water pollution) and psychosocial (i.e. crime, violence, poverty, racism) stressors (Wilson, 2009).

## Salutogens and pathogens in human ecosystems

City and regional planners and community developers may be able to use this ecological framework to improve the health of populations who reside in human ecosystems by tracking the number of and quality of the ecologic features present in the built and social environments (Wilson, 2009). Salutogens are ecologic features of the built and social environments that decrease a population's vulnerability to illness and adverse health outcomes (Antonovsky, 1987; Gee & Payne-Sturges, 2004; MacDonald, 2005; Payne-Sturges, Gee, Crowder, et al., 2006). Salutogens buffer at-risk and susceptible populations from the negative effects of pathogenic environmental exposures and increase opportunities for improvements in health, resiliency, vitality, and social capital (Wilson, 2009). There are several features of human ecosystems that we classify as salutogens, including good housing stocks, parks, medical facilities, schools, open space, supermarkets, recreational facilities, sewer and water infrastructure, equitable and just transportation networks, community gardens, farmers' markets, churches, dentists, and social service organizations (Wilson, 2009). The spatial density, distribution and quality of the salutogens are important indicators of human ecosystem health and points of intervention for improving historically disadvantaged, marginalized, and underserved communities, particularly environmental justice communities. Salutogens constitute the strengths, assets, and resources found in human ecosystems that community development professionals and advocates can use as the foundation for health promotion and prevention in the nation's efforts to eliminate racial/ethnic, socioeconomic-related, and geographic-related health disparities (Wilson, 2009).

Ecologic pathogens are features of the local built and social environments that enhance a population's vulnerability to negative health outcomes (Antonovsky, 1987; Gee & Payne-Sturges, 2004; MacDonald, 2005; Payne-Sturges, Gee, Crowder, et al., 2006), and drives negative health behaviors and lifestyles in a human ecosystem (Wilson, 2009). Ecologic pathogens act as stressors in the neighborhood environment and limit the overall health, sustainability, vitality, and quality of life and levels of social, economic, political, resource and spiritual capital in human ecosystems (Wilson, 2009). There are different categories of pathogens. These pathogens include environmental pathogens or pollutogens (e.g. landfills, incinerators, coal-fired electrical plants, hazardous waste sites, urban blight, locally unwanted land uses, heavily trafficked transportation networks, Superfund sites, waste transfer facilities, industrial corridors), social pathogens (i.e. poverty, structural racism, crime, violence, drug environs), resource pathogens (e.g. poor housing stock, low-quality medical infrastructure, poor sewer and water infrastructure, poor quality roads, fast food restaurants, liquor stores, convenience stores), and economic pathogens (e.g. quick loan facilities, pawn shops, payday lenders) (Wilson, 2009).

In conclusion, the use of this place-centric systems approach will allow us to focus our community development efforts in places with the most need and in the places where the most vulnerable or disadvantaged "reside, work and play" to eliminate disparities in burden, health, well-being, and quality of life. We can use community development programs and initiatives to modify features of the built environment to increase connectivity between different neighborhoods, decrease social isolation, improve neighborhood cohesion, and expand capital. In addition, modification of the built environment and salutogenic infrastructure may increase the accessibility of populations to resources (e.g. parks, medical facilities, grocery stores, churches, social service organizations) within and across spatially-related and unrelated human ecosystems (Wilson, 2009). This is particularly important for marginalized, disadvantaged, and underserved populations (e.g. low-income, persons of color, segregated, elderly, medically vulnerable, immigrants) who may have limited access to health-promoting infrastructure in urban environments and who have been disparately impacted by environmental, economic, and institutional racism and discriminatory policies and laws across multiple generations (Wilson, 2009).

The following case studies provide specific examples of how community-based strategies aim to reduce health disparities by addressing the pathogens described above. These case studies may share a similar goal but are very different with regards to their strategies, collaborations and local context.

## Community-based strategies to address health disparities

### *Jamaica Plain Neighborhood Development Corporation: an effort to improve the economic opportunities of neighborhood residents and diversify of the healthcare workforce*

Boston, Massachusetts is a city that suffers from a high level of racial and ethnic residential segregation. Despite slight decreases in the level of segregation over the past decade, approximately 92% of Boston's black population still lives in just seven of the city's 16 neighborhoods (Boston Public Health Commission, 2005). In order to evenly distribute ethnic and racial diversity throughout the city, 76% of blacks and 60% of Latinos would have to move from their current census tracts (The Boston Disparities Project, 2005).

The high level of racial residential segregation has had a negative impact on Boston's minority neighborhoods and its residents. According to the Mayor's Task Force Blueprint report, of the 22 waste sites in Boston, one-half are in the neighborhood of Roxbury where blacks and Latinos make up the majority of the population (Boston Public Health Commission, 2005). In addition, the Mayor's Task Force Blueprint report stated that lead poisoning is concentrated in the predominately minority communities of Dorchester, Mattapan, and Roxbury. The disproportionate exposure to environmental pollutants has had an effect on poorer children in the City of Boston. Researchers found that, between 1998 and 2002, children under the age of 5 years who lived in Roxbury were nearly twice as likely to be hospitalized for asthma as children in all other neighborhoods of the city (Boston Public Health Commission, 2005). Overall, Latino and black children were 50% more likely to be hospitalized for asthma than whites in this neighborhood (Boston Public Health Commission, 2005).

Racial and ethnic segregation has also no doubt had an effect on the economic opportunities of minority residents. According to The Boston Foundation's (2007) *Boston Indicators Report 2004–2006* there is still a significant amount of disparity in income between whites and racial/ethnic minorities. For example, in 2005 whites had a median household income of $56,627 compared with $31,331 for blacks, $23,424 for Asians, and $20,830 for Latinos (The Boston Foundation, 2007). Household income varied greatly by neighborhood. Residents living in predominately minority neighborhoods such as Roxbury, Dorchester, East Boston, and Mattapan all had household incomes well below the city-wide median of $39,629 (The Boston Foundation, 2007). Unemployment is also high in these neighborhoods. According the 2000 US Census, the neighborhood of Roxbury had an unemployment rate of 11.6% compared with the city, which had an overall employment rate of 7.2% (US Census Bureau, 2000).

The disparities in income and lack of economic opportunity inspired the Jamaica Plain Neighborhood Development Corporation (JPNDC) and its collaborators to develop a grassroots strategy that focuses on training low-wage residents residing in the Boston metropolitan's underserved neighborhoods for jobs within the healthcare sector. JPNDC and their partners formed the Boston Health Care and Research Training Institute (Training Institute), a training model that is focused on two primary goals: improving the educational and employment opportunities of low-wage adults in the healthcare and research industry; and improving the diversity and quality of care of Boston's healthcare institutions. The Training Institute officially began in 2002 as a partnership between eight major employers in the healthcare and research sector. The original partnership included the Boston Private Industry Council, a labor union, four community organizations, and two community colleges. Since its inception, the Training Institute has evolved to include more partners. In just four years the workforce intermediary grew to include 28 partners across the Boston metropolitan area – 11 employers (including all the largest healthcare employers within the Longwood Medical and Academic Area [LMA][1]), 17 organizations of higher education, a healthcare industry association, a labor union, the Boston Private Industry Council (PIC), social service agencies and community organizations. Initially managed by JPNDC in partnership with the Fenway Community Development Corporation (FCDC) and the Mission Hill Network (in February 2008, the Training Institute merged with the Jewish Vocational Service of Boston), the Training Institute provides workforce development training, education and social service support to under-skilled, economically disadvantaged individuals who reside primarily in the Fenway, Jamaica Plain, Mission Hill, and Roxbury neighborhoods of Boston and others from surrounding communities. More specifically, the Training Institute provides education and training programs to individuals who fall into one of the following categories:

- pre-employment job seekers with limited English or education;
- entry-level and mid-level workers lacking the language skills, education, and training needed to move into higher paying healthcare occupations; and
- hospital supervisors who would like assistance in learning how to improve their management skills.

Over the years the Training Institute has worked hard to increase the diversity of Boston's healthcare workforce and increase the economic opportunities of neighborhood residents, especially residents residing in Boston's poorest neighborhoods. Working closely with healthcare administrators, city and regional agencies, local elected officials, community residents, educational institutions, and social service providers, JPNDC and their partners have been successful in placing hundreds of low-wage residents in jobs within Boston's healthcare sector. The Training Institute has also worked with educational institutions and healthcare institutions to form career ladders in administration, patient care, and in technician positions. Most of these jobs pay a livable wage and include healthcare benefits enabling residents to not only improve their income but to gain access to better medical care. Since its inception the Training Institute, with an operating budget of approximately $1 million, has been successful in obtaining hundreds of thousands of dollars in the form of donations and grants from federal, state, and local foundations, government agencies, and the private sector (Boston Social Innovation Forum, 2005).

The early efforts by JPNDC and its collaborators are having a positive impact across the Boston metropolitan area. The Training Institute has become a fixture within the healthcare and research institutions across the Boston metropolitan area as it works to increase the diversity of the workforce and improve the quality of patient care, especially for underserved and minority populations. Moreover, the Training Institute has also focused a significant proportion of its resources reaching out to low-wage, low-skilled residents in an attempt to increase their economic and educational opportunities. These efforts have resulted in the Boston Redevelopment Authority (BRA) to require all developers or healthcare institutions planning development within Boston's LMA to make "an assessment of current and projected workforce needs, and to work with the BRA and the Office of Jobs and Community Services (JCS) staff to formulate a workforce development plan to address those needs" as part of the development review process (Boston Redevelopment Authority, 2003). The BRA's LMA Interim Guidelines specifically mention that it is expected that LMA institution's workforce development plans would include an increased investment in the Training Institute (Boston Redevelopment Authority, 2003). This strategy of tying development to community benefits (in the form of economic, educational, and access to medical care) helps to ensure that the poorest and least healthy residents residing in the Boston metropolitan area will have some opportunities to improve their quality of life.

In 2005 the City of Boston under the leadership of Mayor Menino released several reports and data documenting racial and ethnic disparities in the city and discussed recommended strategies to address those disparities. The initiative known as The Disparities Project is an effort to reduce racial and ethnic health disparities and to bring Boston's institutions and organizations together in order to promote fairness, equality and good health for all residents (Boston Public Health Commission, 2005; National Association of County and City Health Officials, 2011). Improving the diversity of the healthcare workforce is one of the major goals of the initiative. In an effort to improve the quality of healthcare and address workforce diversity, The Disparities Project has included the Training Institute as one of its local best practices (currently The Disparities Project oversees the implementation of 33 hospital and community-based projects in all neighborhoods in Boston) (National Association of County and City Health Officials, 2011). The hope is that, with time, efforts such as the Training Institute will be effective in diversifying the Boston metropolitan area's healthcare workforce, which will result in more culturally competent care and an overall improvement in service delivery for patients. Although a comprehensive analysis of the Training Institute's impact at increasing the economic opportunity of lower-skilled, economically disadvantaged residents has not been completed, and nor has one documenting the increases in diversity of Boston's healthcare workforce and its impact at reducing health disparities, it is clear that under the direction of JPNDC and its collaborators it has been able to begin making a difference at the local, city-wide, and regional level – only time will tell of how much of a difference it has made.

## ReGenesis: an environmental justice organization's revitalization efforts in South Carolina

The City of Spartanburg is located in northwest South Carolina and has population of 40,000 with 50% black and 50% white (US Environmental Protection Agency [USEPA], 2003, 2006). This former "textile town" has undergone a transformation from its revitalized downtown to the high concentration of international business firms within the city limits (Fleming, 2004; USEPA, 2003, 2006). However, the Arkwright and Forest Park neighborhoods, two predominantly black neighborhoods with a combined population of almost 5000 residents located just beyond the City's downtown, have not benefited from these revitalization efforts (Fleming, 2004; USEPA, 2003, 2006). The closing of local mills and plants and the lack of zoning regulations and land-use controls (Fleming, 2004; Habisreutinger & Gunderson, 2006; USEPA, 2003, 2006) have left the population poor (25% in poverty), underemployed (10% unemployment) (USEPA, 2003, 2006) and negatively impacted by environmental injustice, underdevelopment, and limited access to health-promoting resources.

The residents live in a riskscape made of several environmental pathogens including the 40-acre International Mineral and Chemicals (IMC) fertilizer plant (a Superfund site), the Arkwright dump, the 30-acre former municipal landfill (a Superfund site), Rhodia chemical plant (in operation), Mt. Vernon textile mill (in operation), and six brownfields (Fleming, 2004; Habisreutinger & Gunderson, 2006; ReGenesis, 2008; USEPA, 2003, 2006). Approximately 4700 residents lived within one mile of the IMC site, 200 live within a quarter of a mile of the landfill, and several residents live adjacent to the Rhodia plant (Fleming, 2004; ReGenesis, 2008; USEPA, 2003, 2006). Due to these exposures, there is a high rate of cancer, particularly bone, colon, and lung cancer; high rates of respiratory illnesses, adult mortality, infant mortality, miscarriages, and birth defects; and in 2000 alone over 60 people died (ReGenesis, 2008; USEPA, 2003, 2006). In addition to these problems, neighborhood residents had poor transportation infrastructure, limited sewer and water services, lack of access to medical care, public safety issues, few economic opportunities, and declining property values (USEPA, 2003, 2006).

In 1997, Harold Mitchell, a resident concerned about the environmental contamination in his community, personally impacted by the loss of family members and his own health issues, and passionate about revitalizing his community, began organizing community meetings and forums to discuss environmental justice and health issues in the community (Fleming, 2004; ReGenesis, 2008; USEPA, 2003, 2006). These meetings began to empower local residents and motivate efforts by the government and industry to clean up the contaminated Superfund sites and brownfields, and later the community-driven collaboration became known as the "ReGenesis Project." In 1998, ReGenesis evolved into an environmental justice organization with official 501c3 status under the leadership of Harold Mitchell (Fleming, 2004; ReGenesis, 2008; USEPA, 2003, 2006). ReGenesis built an environmental justice partnership with the City of Spartanburg, Spartanburg County, EPA Region 4 Office of Environmental Justice, the South Carolina Department of Health and Environmental Control, Spartanburg Housing Authority, Spartanburg County's Community and Economic Development Department, local industry, and the University of South Carolina Upstate based on collaborative problem-solving principles to address the impacts of the brownfields, Superfund sites, and other environmental pathogens on local health and adopt strategies that could be employed to revitalize the Arkwright–Forest Park neighborhoods (USEPA, 2003, 2006).

With help from EPA Region 4, ReGenesis was designated one of the first 15 national demonstration projects of the Federal Interagency Working Group on Environmental Justice in 2000, which gave ReGenesis access to financial resources ($20,000) and technical experts and information (USEPA, 2003, 2006). With this designation, new funding was made available and local, state, and federal agencies began to understand that immediate action was needed in the Arkwright–Forest Park neighborhoods to save and improve lives (USEPA, 2003, 2006). The County of Spartanburg was awarded $200,000 through the EPA's Brownfield Initiative to perform site assessments of the brownfields on behalf of ReGenesis (Habisreutinger & Gunderson, 2006; ReGenesis 2008; USEPA, 2003, 2006). The brownfields assessment found contamination and led to government agencies providing additional funding to clean up the sites for redevelopment (Habisreutinger & Gunderson, 2006; ReGenesis, 2008; USEPA, 2003, 2006). For example, the South Carolina Department of Health and Environmental Control provided a $490,000 grant for brownfields redevelopment (ReGenesis, 2008; USEPA, 2003, 2006). HUD provided a $650,000 grant to ReGenesis and the City to clean up the brownfields and blighted properties and to help with neighborhood redevelopment efforts (ReGenesis, 2008; USEPA, 2003, 2006). In addition, the City of Spartanburg signed a cooperative agreement with the EPA to assess the nature and extent of contamination at the Arkwright Dump site, review the human and environmental health risks, and examine clean-up alternatives (Habisreutinger & Gunderson, 2006; ReGenesis, 2008; USEPA, 2003, 2006). The City of Spartanburg received $1.2 million dollars and used it to conduct water quality monitoring and remediation at the site (ReGenesis, 2008; USEPA, 2003, 2006). Eventually, the industrial owner of the property provided nearly $3 million in funding to the EPA for oversight, assessment, and remediation of the site (ReGenesis, 2008; Habisreutinger & Gunderson, 2006; USEPA, 2003, 2006).

The success of ReGenesis in working with its collaborative partner for assessment, cleanup, and redevelopment of brownfields and other industrial sites as part of the community revitalization efforts led to additional efforts to improve the salutogenic infrastructure in the Arkwright–Forest Park neighborhoods. ReGenesis received a US Department of Transportation (DOT) appropriation for $2 million dollars for road design and construction in order to connect the Arkwright–Forest Park neighborhoods to the greater Spartanburg community and improve access to emergency care services (ReGenesis, 2008; USEPA, 2003, 2006). ReGenesis also received $102 million dollars in HOPE VI funding to build energy-efficient, affordable housing and improve safety in the community (ReGenesis, 2008; USEPA, 2003, 2006). One of ReGenesis' greatest successes is the establishment of its Community Health Center (CHC) in 2003 through a $645,000 grant from the Department of Health and Human Services (ReGenesis 2008; USEPA, 2003, 2006). This health center provided the only source of care when it was established for many residents in the medically underserved community. The CHC is one of only 19 federally approved community health centers in the state of South Carolina and currently provides a medical home for approximately 14,000 patients (USEPA, 2003, 2006). The CHC is at the core of the long-term development and revitalization plans for the community.

Due to the collaborative effort of more than 200 agencies who contributed to the Environmental Justice partnership, the ReGenesis project has acquired $141 million in funds as of 2006 (USEPA, 2006). ReGenesis has expanded its community development and revitalization efforts to pediatric health, development of minority-owned businesses and job training through the ReGenesis Economic Development Organization, and urban greenways (ReGenesis 2008; USEPA, 2003, 2006). ReGenesis' use of the collaborative problem-solving framework has been celebrated by the EPA, who named it a model community-based environmental justice organization (ReGenesis, 2008; USEPA, 2003, 2006). Harold Mitchell has taken ReGenesis' community development and revitalization agenda to the South Carolina House of Representatives, where he has authored several affordable housing bills and environmental justice legislation to help improve the lives of underserved South Carolinians (ReGenesis, 2008).

## *The West End Revitalization Association: a story of success in North Carolina*

Mebane, NC, is a small town located between Burlington and Chapel Hill, North Carolina. In this small community, black residents are concentrated in four historic neighborhoods (West End, White Level, Buckhorn/Perry Hill, and East End) (Heaney, Wilson, & Wilson, 2007; West End Revitalization Association [WERA], 2002, 2008; Wilson, Bumpass, Wilson, & Snipes, 2008; Wilson, Heaney, & Wilson, 2010; Wilson, Wilson, Heaney, & Cooper, 2007/2008). The WERA is a community-based organization fighting against environmental injustice, inequities in community development and planning, built environment insults, and health disparities in West End, White Level, and Buckhorn/Perry Hill (Heaney et al., 2007; Wilson, Bumpass, Wilson, & Snipes, 2008; Wilson, Heaney, & Wilson, 2010; Wilson, Wilson, Heaney, & Cooper, 2007). These neighborhoods have many low-income and elderly residents who are descendants of slaves and own land and property in Mebane passed down across multiple generations (Heaney et al., 2007; WERA, 2002, 2008; Wilson, Bumpass, Wilson, & Snipes, 2008; Wilson, Heaney, & Wilson, 2010; Wilson, Wilson, Heaney, & Cooper, 2007). The West End community hosts an old garbage dump, city landfill, and Mebane's sewage treatment plant (WERA, 2002, 2008). The West End community had been denied access to municipal sewer and water services even though residential health had been impaired by foul odors and air pollution from the sewage treatment plant, garbage dump, landfill, and a 50–100% failure rate of backyard septic systems (Heaney et al., 2007; WERA, 2002, 2008; Wilson, Bumpass, Wilson, & Snipes, 2008; Wilson, Heaney, & Wilson, 2010; Wilson, Wilson, Heaney, & Cooper, 2007). In addition, these neighborhoods are disparately impacted by a closed furniture production factory and underground storage tanks leaking carcinogenic compounds (e.g. benzene, xylene) (Heaney et al., 2007; WERA, 2002, 2008; Wilson, Bumpass, Wilson, & Snipes, 2008; Wilson, Heaney, & Wilson, 2010; Wilson, Wilson, Heaney, & Cooper, 2007).

The WERA was founded in 1994 as a community development corporation and incorporated as a North Carolina 501(c)3 non-profit in 1995 when the North Carolina Department of Transportation (NCDOT) released plans to construct the 119-bypass through two African-American communities (West End and White Level) (Heaney et al., 2007; WERA, 2002, 2008; Wilson, Bumpass, Wilson, & Snipes, 2008; Wilson, Heaney, & Wilson, 2010; Wilson, Wilson, Heaney, & Cooper, 2007). NCDOT plans to extend the 5-mile 119-bypass from I-85/40 north into the planned 27-mile interstate eight-lane highway corridor through White Level to Dansville, Virginia (Heaney et al., 2007; WERA, 2002, 2008; Wilson, Bumpass, Wilson, & Snipes, 2008; Wilson, Heaney, & Wilson, 2010; Wilson, Wilson, Heaney, & Cooper,

2007). Through right-of-way acquisition and displacement, the NCDOT planned to pay from $25,000 to $52,000 for houses regardless of their replacement value. Century old churches, small businesses, and a Masonic Temple would not be compensated. For over 15 years, local governments and the NCDOT planned the project without community knowledge or input (Heaney et al., 2007; WERA, 2002; Wilson, Bumpass, Wilson, & Snipes, 2008; Wilson, Heaney, & Wilson, 2010; Wilson, Wilson, Heaney, & Cooper, 2007). Community involvement and public hearings were held on the 119-bypass after WERA and African-American residents filed a joint Environment Justice Executive Order 12898 and Title VI of Civil Right Act complaint in 1999 at the US Department of Justice. In 1999, the NCDOT transportation corridor was placed on moratorium by the Federal Highway Administration until mitigation and corrective actions were implemented (Heaney et al., 2007; WERA, 2002; Wilson, Bumpass, Wilson, & Snipes, 2008; Wilson, Heaney, & Wilson, 2010; Wilson, Wilson, Heaney, & Cooper, 2007).

To address environmental justice, community development and planning, built environment, and health disparity issues, the WERA moved from being just a community development corporation to a community-based environmental protection organization and developed the community-owned and managed research (COMR) approach in order to empower WERA board, staff, members, and residents and use research to obtain redress for issues to impact WERA neighborhoods (Heaney et al., 2007; Wilson, Bumpass, Wilson, & Snipes, 2008; Wilson, Heaney, & Wilson, 2010; Wilson, Wilson, Heaney, & Cooper, 2007). The COMR approach is an evolved version of the community-based participatory research framework that focuses in parity in management of scientific research and equity in research funding. The use of COMR has increased community awareness and understanding of research related to public health, promoted public and civic engagement, enhanced public trust in community facilitation of research and ownership of databases, increased scientific literacy and community-driven research on environmental issues, and empowered community members (Heaney et al., 2007; Wilson et al., 2007).

In addition to the development of the COMR approach, the WERA developed a long-term multi-stakeholder collaborative partnership based on the EPA's environmental justice collaborative problem-solving principles (Heaney et al., 2007; Wilson et al., 2007). This partnership includes partners from the government, universities, health sector, community development and revitalization professionals, non-profits, environmental justice communities, and funders (Heaney et al., 2007; Wilson et al., 2007). These partners worked together on several workgroups using conflict resolution, resource leveraging and mobilization, consensus building and other collaborative principles (Heaney et al., 2007; Wilson et al., 2007) and other initiatives to address built environment, development, and health issues in WERA neighborhoods. These partners have been instrumental in sustaining the collaborative partnership over a period of 10 years and improved WERA's ability to address issues in WERA communities and other historically marginalized, disadvantaged, and underserved communities in Mebane, North Carolina, and nationally.

WERA's COMR research was funded by three grants: an EPA Environment Justice Small Grant ($15,000), University of North Carolina (Chapel Hill) EXPORT health disparities grant ($10,000), and EPA's Office of Environmental Justice Collaborative Problem-Solving grant ($100,000) (Heaney et al., 2007; Wilson et al., 2007). The experience, knowledge, and skills gained have helped the WERA leverage reduction and removal of hazards that create disproportionate and adverse public health risks under EPA's Safe Drinking Water Act, Clean Water Act, Clean Air Act, Solid Waste Disposal Act, and Toxic Substance Control Act (Heaney et al., 2007; Wilson et al., 2007). WERA's research on basic amenities (e.g. sewer and water infrastructure) documented Escherichia coli and fecal coliforms in residential well water, municipal drinking water, and surface waters that exceeded EPA's Safe Drinking Water Act and Clean Water Act standards (Heaney et al., 2007; WERA, 2002, 2008; Wilson, Bumpass, Wilson, & Snipes, 2008; Wilson, Heaney, & Wilson, 2010; Wilson, Wilson, Heaney, & Cooper, 2007). The efforts of the collaborative-problem solving partnership to obtain basic amenities led to the first-time sewer line installation for 91 homes in the West End community for only $75 per unit funded by block grants and City of Mebane matching, the connection of many WERA households to municipal water services, first-time paving of neighborhood streets, installation of gutters, removal of dilapidated and blighted housing, and leveraging of resources to continue the moratorium of the 119-bypass construction and changing of the highway plans that no longer disproportionately impact a large number of low-income black residents (Heaney et al., 2007; WERA, 2002, 2008; Wilson, Bumpass, Wilson, & Snipes, 2008; Wilson, Heaney, & Wilson, 2010; Wilson, Wilson, Heaney, & Cooper, 2007). WERA's collaborative environmental justice partnership, community-driven research, and use of Title VI of the Civil Rights Act to obtain compliance with environmental laws and public health statutes and basic amenities is a great model for other communities burdened by environmental injustice, uneven development, planning inequities, and health disparities.

## Conclusion

Numerous research studies up until now have documented the deleterious impacts of racial residential segregation within metropolitan areas across the United States. Residential segregation more often than not creates neighborhoods of poverty that lack access to first-rate medical care, affordable housing, quality education, healthy food, and adequate infrastructure. Instead, poorer and minority residents forced to live in segregated communities are often left to reside in communities that are unsafe and have high levels of environmental pollutants. The persistent exposure to negative social, economic, and environmental conditions leads to poorer health outcomes for disadvantaged and minority populations, thus contributing to racial and ethnic health disparities.

If we as a nation are going to close the racial and ethnic health disparities gap that currently exists in this country, this will require a comprehensive framework that considers ecologic features of the built and social environment to enhance community development in unserved and underserved communities hurt by health disparities. As we have already mentioned, this approach must focus on understanding how context, place, and local socioenvironmental conditions impact the health of populations and individuals. A large portion of this work, as demonstrated by our community development cases, must be done at the grassroots community level. Community organizations and institutions are well-equipped to understand the challenges, assets, concerns, and potential opportunities that exist in local neighborhoods and are positioned to begin improving and modifying the health and quality of our neighborhoods.

An example of a place-based strategy that works to create healthy neighborhoods by using such a comprehensive approach is The Building Healthy Communities program. Launched in 2010 by The California Endowment, the largest health foundation in the state, the Building Healthy Communities program is a 10-year, $1 billion program to invest in 14 communities in both urban and rural areas across California.[2] The goal is to improve the health of these underserved and vulnerable communities by "improving employment opportunities, education, housing, neighborhood safety, unhealthy environmental conditions, access to healthy foods and more" (The California Endowment, 2010). A key goal of the Building Healthy Communities program is for it to be community-driven; it ultimately seeks to create communities for children where they are healthy, safe and able to learn (The California Endowment, 2010).

In addition to comprehensive place-based strategies such as The California Endowment's Building Healthy Communities program, a number of communities have also begun to rely on health impact assessments (HIAs) in order to improve neighborhood or community health. HIAs bring together public input, available data and a range of quantitative and qualitative methods to understand the potential health consequences of a proposed program, project or policy (Health Impact Project 2011[3]). In San Francisco, California, the University of California at Berkeley Health Impact Group, with funding from the Centers for Disease Control and through the federal HOPE VI program, completed a public draft of a retrospective HIA of the redevelopment of two public housing sites (Bernal Dwellings and North Beach Place). The HIA was interested in how redevelopment of public housing impacted the health of residents of two public housing sites in San Francisco (UC Berkeley Health Impact Group, 2009).

Finally in an effort to create healthier communities, a number of cities across California are using their general plan update process to transform their land use and built environment. Some cities, such as the cities of Anderson, Chino, and Richmond, California, are including a separate health element in their general plan and other cities are adding health goals and policies in various general plan elements (Healthy Eating Active Living Cities Campaign, 2011). These efforts are the first step towards what is needed to build healthy communities and reduce the level of health disparities.

As the institutions behind these programs and strategies recognize, real change in our communities requires that community institutions and local residents in partnership with public health agencies, planning institutions, social service agencies, government, non-profit organizations, and the private sector to confront the institutionalized racism and discrimination that creates disadvantaged communities across our metropolitan areas with unequal access to economic, educational, and social opportunities. In addition, addressing institutional racism and discrimination can lead to improved neighborhood environments with more equitable development and planning so that poorer residents are not exposed to an unjust amount of environmental pollutants and land uses. Only a comprehensive community-centered strategy is capable of positively impacting the lifestyles, health behaviors, health outcomes, and quality of life of populations who reside, work, or play in disadvantaged, historically marginalized, and underserved communities.

**Notes**

1. The Longwood Medical and Academic Area is located on 213-acre site with 24 institutions and has 15.4 million square feet of development. Each day more than 40,000 employees and 18,200 students provide medical care, conduct research, teach, attend school, or support these functions (Medical Academic and Scientific Community Organization, 2008).

2. See http://www.calendow.org/healthycommunities/
3. The Health Impact Project, a collaboration of the Robert Wood Johnson Foundation and The Pew Charitable Trusts, is a national initiative designed to promote the use of HIAs as a decision-making tool for policy-makers. See http://www.healthimpactproject.org/

**References**

Acevedo-Garcia, D., Osypuk, T.L., McArdle, N., & Williams, D.R. (2008). Toward a policy-relevant analysis of geographic and racial/ethnic disparities in child health. *Health Affairs, 14*(2), 321–333.

Ahmed, A.T., Mohammed, S.A., & Williams, D.R. (2007). Racial discrimination & health: Pathways & evidence. *Indian Journal of Medical Research, 126,* 318–327.

Alba, R.D., & Logan, J.R. (1993)Minority proximity to whites in suburbs: An individual-level analysis of segregation. *American Journal of Sociology, 98,* 1388–1427.

Antonovsky, A. (1987). *Unravelling the mystery of health: How people manage stress and stay well.* San Francisco, CA: Jossey-Bass.

The Boston Disparities Project. (2006). *Boston Public Health Commission.* Boston, MA. Retrieved from http://www.naccho.org/topics/modelpractices/database/practice.cfm?practice ID=318

Boston Public Health Commission. (2005). *Mayor's Task Force blueprint: A plan to eliminate racial and ethnic disparities in health.* Retrieved from http://www.bphc.org/director/disp_blueprint.asp

Boston Redevelopment Authority. (2003). *LMA Interim Guidelines.* Boston, MA. www.boston redevelopmentauthority.org/pdf/.../LMA_Int_Guidelines.pdf

Boston Social Innovation Forum. (2005). *Boston Health Care and Research Training Institute Prospectus.* http://www.rootcause.org/performance-measurement/profiles/boston-health-care-and-research-training-institute

Brulle, R.J., & Pellow, D.N. (2006). Environmental justice: Human health and environmental inequalities. *Annual Review of Public Health, 27,* 103–124.

Center for Disease Control. (2010). *National vital statistics reports* (Vol. 58, No. 19). Atlanta, GA: Centers for Disease Control.

Corburn, J. (2009). *Toward the healthy city: People, places, and the politics of urban planning.* Cambridge, MA. MIT Press.

Dreier, P., Mollenkopf, J., & Swanstrom, T. (2004). *Place matters: Metropolitics for the twenty-first century* (2nd ed., rev.). Lawrence, KS: University of Kansas Press.

Fitzpartick, K., & LaGory, M. (2000). *Unhealthy places.* London: Routledge.

Fleming, C. (2004). When environmental justice hits the local agenda: A profile of Spartanburg and Spartanburg County, South Carolina. *PM Magazine, 86*(5), 1–10.

Frug, G.E. (1999). *City making: Building community without building walls.* Princeton, NJ: Princeton University Press.

Gee, G., & Payne-Sturges, D. (2004). Environmental health disparities: A framework integrating psychosocial and environmental concepts. *Environmental Health Perspectives, 112*(17), 1645–1653.

Habisreutinger, P., & Gunderson, D.E. (2006). Real estate reuse opportunities within the ReGenesis project area: A case study. *International Journal of Construction Education and Research, 2*(1), 53–63.

Hahn, J.A. (1992). The state of Federal health statistics on racial and ethnic groups. *JAMA, 267,* 268–271.

Healthy Eating Active Living Cities Campaign. (2011). *HEAL homepage.* Retrieved March 7, 2011, from http://www.healcitiescampaign.org/index.html

Heaney, C.D., Wilson, S.M., & Wilson, O.R. (2007). The West End Revitalization Association's community-owned and -managed research model: Development, implementation, and action. *Progress in Community Health Partnerships: Research, Education and Action, 1*(4), 339–350.

Hummer, R.A., Rogers, R.G., Nam, C.B., & LeClere, F.B. (1999). Race/ethnicity, nativity, and U.S. adult mortality. *Social Science Quarterly, 80,* 136–153.

Hutson, M.A., Kaplan, G.A., Ranjit, N., & Mujahid, M. (2011). Metropolitan fragmentation and health disparities: Is there a link? *Manuscript submitted for publication.*

Institute of Medicine. (2002, March). *Unequal treatment: Confronting racial and ethnic disparities in healthcare*. Washington, D.C.: National Academies Press.

LaVeist, T.A. (1993). Separation, poverty, and empowerment: Health consequences for African Americans. *Milbank Quarterly, 73*(1), 41–64.

Lopez, R. (2004). Income inequality and self-rated health in US metropolitan areas: A multilevel analysis. *Social Science & Medicine, 59*, 2409–2419.

MacDonald, J.J. (2005). *Environmental for health: A salutogenic approach*. Sterling, VA: Earthscan.

Massey, D. (2004). Segregation and stratification: A biosocial perspective. *Du Bois Review, 1*(1), 7–25.

Massey, D.S., & Denton, N.A. (1993). *American apartheid: Segregation and the Making of the underclass*. Cambridge, MA: Harvard University Press.

Medical Academic and Scientific Community Organization. (2008). Retrieved from http://www.masco.org/thelma/about-lma

Morello-Frosch, R., & Lopez, R. (2006). The riskscape and the color line: Examining the role of segregation in environmental health disparities. *Environmental Research, 102*, 181–196.

National Association of County and City Health Officials. (2011). *NACCHO model practices*. Retrieved March 8, 2011, from http://www.naccho.org/topics/modelpractices/

Payne-Sturges, D., Gee, G.C., Crowder, K., Hurley, B.J., Lee, C., Morello-Frosch, R., et al. (2006). Workshop summary: Connecting social and environmental factors to measure and track environmental health disparities. *Environmental Research, 102*, 146–153.

ReGenesis. (2008). *Environmental justice demonstration project: Community revitalization through partnerships*. Retrieved May 20, 2008, from http://www.regenesisproject.org/

Singh, G.K., & Yu, S.M. (1996). Adverse pregnancy outcomes: Differences Between U.S. and foreign-born women in major U.S. racial and ethnic groups. *American Journal of Public Health, 86*, 837–843.

Soobader, M., Cubbin, C., & Gee, G.C. (2006). Levels of analysis for the study of environmental health disparities: the role of place and social theory. *Environmental Research, 102*, 172–180.

Sorlie, P.D., Rogot, E., & Johnson, N.J. (1993). Validity of demographic characteristics on the death certificate. *Epidemiology, 3*, 181–184.

Sze, J. (2007). *Noxious New York: The racial politics of urban health and environmental justice*. Cambridge, MA: MIT Press.

The Boston Foundation. (2007). *The Boston indicators project report 2004–2006*. Retrieved from http://www.bostonindicators.org/uploadedFiles/Indicators/Indicators2006/Homepage/2004-06_IndicatorsRpt.pdf

The California Endowment. (2011). *Building Healthy Communities program*. Retrieved March 7, 2011, from http://www.calendow.org/healthycommunities/

UC Berkeley Health Impact Group. (2009, November). *HOPE VI to HOPE SF, San Francisco public housing redevelopment: A health impact assessment*. Berkeley, CA: University of California. Retrieved from http://www.hiacollaborative.org/case-studies

US Census Bureau. (2000). Retrieved from www.uscensus.gov

US Environmental Protection Agency. (2003). *Towards an environmental justice collaborative model: Case studies of six partnerships used to address environmental justice issues in communities* (EPA/100-R-03-002). Washington, DC: USEPA.

US Environmental Protection Agency. (2006). *EPA's environmental justice collaborative problem-solving model* (EPA 300-R-06-002). Washington, DC: USEPA.

West End Revitalization Association. (2002). *Failing septic systems and contaminated well waters: African-American communities in Mebane, North Carolina* (Final Report No. EPA #4EAD/EJ). Washington DC: US Environmental Protection Agency.

West End Revitalization Association. (2008). *WERA homepage*. Retrieved May 27, 2008, from http://www.wera-nc.org/

Williams, D.R. (1999). Race, socioeconomic status, and health: The added effects of racism and discrimination. *Annals New York Academy of Sciences, 896*, 173–188.

Williams, D.R., & Collins, C. (2001). Racial residential segregation: A fundamental cause of racial disparities in health. *Public Health Reports, 116*(5), 404–416.

Williams, D.R., & Jackson, P.B. (2005). Social sources of racial disparities in health. *Health Affairs, 24*(2), 325–334.

Wilson, O.R., Bumpass, N.G., Wilson, O.M., & Snipes, M.H. (2008), The West End Revitalization Association (WERA)'s right to basic amenities movement: Voice and language of ownership and management of public health solutions in Mebane, North Carolina. *Progress in Community Health Partnerships*, 2(3), 237–243.

Wilson, S.M. (2009). A holistic framework to study and address environmental justice and community health issues. *Environmental Justice*, 2(1), 1–9.

Wilson, S.M., Cooper, J., Heaney, C.D., & Wilson, O.R. (2008). Built environment issues in unserved and underserved African-American neighborhoods in North Carolina. *Environmental Justice*, 1(2), 63–72.

Wilson, S.M., Heaney, C.D., & Wilson, O.R. (2010). Governance structures and the lack of basic amenities: Can community engagement be effectively used to address environmental injustice in underserved black communities? *Environmental Justice*, 3(4), 125–133.

Wilson, S.M., Wilson, O.R., Heaney, C.D., & Cooper, C. (2007). Use of EPA collaborative problem-solving model to obtain environmental justice in North Carolina. *Progress in Community Health Partnerships: Research, Education and Action*, 1(4), 327–338.

Wilson, S.M., Wilson, O.R., Heaney, C.D., & Cooper, J. (2007/2008). Community-driven environmental protection: Reducing the P.A.I.N. of the built environment in low-income African-American communities in North Carolina. *Social Justice in Context*, 3, 41–58.

Wilson, W.J. (1996). *When work disappears: The world of the urban poor*. New York: Knopf.

# Smart growth principles and the management of urban sprawl

Robert Blair and Gerard Wellman

*University of Nebraska Omaha, Public Administration/Urban Studies, USA*

> Employing a policy communities framework to compare implementation efforts among a set of cities, this study seeks to answer the question: do public policies advocated by the Smart Growth Network, a coalition of organizations promoting a specific policy agenda, provide cities with policy initiatives, guidance, and tools that manage urban sprawl. In other words, do policy advocacy coalitions promote policies that actually manage sprawl? The authors, using two studies that ranked metropolitan areas using indexes that measured changes in sprawl, collected and analyzed planning documents and other public policy initiatives from four moderately sized, Midwestern, metropolitan statistical areas: Omaha, Nebraska; Davenport, Iowa; Wichita, Kansas; and Springfield, Missouri. They found that specific policy strategies consistent with Smart Growth were important to managing sprawl, but also important is the overall implementation philosophies of the cities toward growth management.

## Introduction

Urban sprawl persists as one of the more intractable issues facing local governments. While research demonstrates the social and economic costs of sprawl (Black & Curtis, 1993; Burchell, 1998; Katz & Bradley, 1999; Porter, 1997; Squires, 2002), large tracts of green space continue to disappear at the periphery of most large cities. Historically, sprawl consumes land at almost three times the rate of population growth (Rusk, 2000), and since 1960 the percentage of new land consumed by metropolitan areas has increased dramatically (Stoel, 1999). Urban sprawl raises concerns about social equity in metropolitan areas including the delivery of services and jobs and the environmental conditions in older, poorly maintained neighborhoods (Ciscel, 2001). Left behind in decaying inner cities, the socioeconomically disadvantaged endure a poverty rate twice that of suburban rates, reduced mobility, and isolation from goods and services (Katz & Bradley, 1999). In spite of the importance of social justice and fairness considerations for urban planning, David Harvey (2009, p. 9) notes that they have been ignored within the field. Some label urban sprawl as one of the top three "threats to community," in the United States (Williamson, Imbroscio, & Alperovitz, 2005, p. 303), while others see the propagation of sprawl through a political economy lens as a form of institutional racism and socioeconomic exclusionary practices (Bartle & Wellman, 2010; Harvey, 2009; Palen, 2008).

Suburban sprawl has many implications for urban development, transportation, community development, and public health. When low-density development patterns on the fringes of metropolitan areas are encouraged, public transportation becomes more difficult to provide (Boschken, 2002) and more expensive to maintain. Reliance on the personal automobile, a direct consequence of separating land uses and low-density developments, encourages road building at higher rates. For example, in Omaha, Nebraska, the city spent $179 per capita on roads in 2002 compared with $30 per capita on transit, and 95% of road projects in the Omaha metropolitan area in 2009 were in low-density suburban areas (Bartle & Wellman, 2010). Resulting disinvestment in the inner-city disenfranchises residents, compounds social problems, and has prompted entire academic research areas of environmental justice and transit equity.

In spite of this awareness, research shows wide variation in response to urban sprawl and growth by city officials (El Nasser & Overberg, 2001; Fulton, Pendall, Nguyen, & Harrison, 2001). There is evidence of some success in managing sprawl. What factors account for this variation? Do policies espoused by the Smart Growth Network help address urban sprawl? Is adherence to Smart Growth Network policies associated with higher sprawl management rankings? Most importantly, do advocates of growth management provide local government officials with the policy guidance and strategies to better control urban sprawl?

This paper attempts to address these questions by examining urban sprawl management approaches in four mid-sized, Midwestern cities. Utilizing two studies that ranked metropolitan areas using indices to measure changes in sprawl, this study strives to determine whether public policies advocated by the Smart Growth Network (2010) provide the cities studied here with policy initiatives, guidance, and tools that better manage urban sprawl. In other words, do policy advocacy coalitions, like the Smart Growth Network, promote policies that are applicable and usable to policy-makers? The authors collected and analyzed data from four Midwestern, metropolitan statistical areas (MSAs) – Davenport, Iowa; Omaha, Nebraska; Springfield, Missouri; and Wichita, Kansas – compared the policies and efforts to address sprawl, examined the types of policy approaches, and observed the efficacy of Smart Growth principles.

**The smart growth network: an advocacy coalition**

Like most public policy areas, urban sprawl and growth management policy exists within a complex environment of policy advocates, actors, and institutions. Often referred to as policy communities, they perform a critical function in the policy process, providing "forums where actors discuss policy issues and persuade and bargain in pursuit of their interests" (Howlett & Ramesh, 1995, p. 51). Policy formulation and implementation occurs within policy communities, although the contentious nature of many advocacy coalitions makes such communities more complex. The Smart Growth Network exemplifies an advocacy coalition: it is a collection of organizations operating within the urban growth policy community promoting a specific set of policy strategies to accommodate the pressures of urban growth.

The urban sprawl policy community meets the standard of a complex policy community, "characterized by diverse and strong opinions on policy goals and program proposals by subsystem actors, varying degrees of technical capacity among government units, and the overriding presence and influence of fierce market forces in the policy environment" (Blair, 2001, p. 105). In addition to large national coalitions like the Smart Growth Network (Allen, 1999; Danielsen, Lang, & Fulton, 1998) and Smart Growth America (Ewing, Pendall, & Chen, 2002), small non-profit organizations like The Growth Management Institute advocate growth management policies aimed at creating sustainable development with the preservation of environmental quality as a stated goal (Porter, 1997). This complex and diverse policy community contains stakeholders who support restrictions on urban growth as well as those who declare that urban growth should only be "regulated" by the forces of a competitive market place (Gordon & Richardson, 2001). The latter group downplays the benefits of growth management policies (Downs, 1999), and criticizes zoning and subdivision laws, believing them to be obstacles to appropriate growth and development (Powell, 2000).

The Smart Growth Network, a coalition of more than 40 national, state, and local organizations working to minimize low-density, auto-dependent development, advocates a set of policies designed to overcome problems associated with sprawl by rethinking the costs associated with decaying inner-city infrastructure, reverse commuting, abandoned brownfields, disappearing green space and agricultural land on city fringes (Smart Growth Network, 2010). Smart Growth advocates focus on restoring city centers and creating a "town-centered," pedestrian-friendly urban environment that offers a mix of housing and commercial uses while preserving natural areas. The Network promotes a set of principles to guide economical and environmentally responsible development, encouraging local governments to:

(1) Create ranges of housing opportunities and choices
(2) Create walkable neighborhoods
(3) Encourage community and stakeholder collaboration
(4) Foster distinctive, attractive communities with a strong sense of place
(5) Make development decisions predictable, fair and cost-effective
(6) Mix land uses
(7) Preserve open space, farmland, natural beauty, and critical environmental areas
(8) Provide a variety of transportation choices
(9) Strengthen and direct development toward existing communities
(10) Take advantage of compact building design (Smart Growth Network, 2010)

Advocacy coalitions, like the Smart Growth Network, promote specific policy agendas. Their website[1] lists a variety of methods to encourage policy-makers to adopt their policy proposals, including books, pamphlets, educational forums, workshops, and speakers. Advocacy coalitions play an important role in formulating public policy: promoting policy alternatives, providing technical information, and engaging in policy education. Research on advocacy coalitions have focused on the structure of the coalitions, the nature of their policy proposals, and the process of policy learning in specific policy areas (Sabatier & Jenkins-Smith, 1999). This paper examines the policy education function of advocacy coalitions.

## Measuring sprawl and the effectiveness of growth management

Urban sprawl is a complex concept, with measurement presenting a formidable obstacle to comparative policy research. Like the policy areas of housing, economic development, and environmental protection, policies governing, promulgating, or restricting sprawl do not affect all communities equally; in other words, benefits and costs are not evenly shared by all stakeholders and this has resultant implications for theorists concerned about equity, fairness, and justice (Boschken, 2002; Logan & Molotch, 1987). The multi-dimensional nature of sprawl adds to the complexity of measurement. Galster et al. identified eight distinct benchmarks of land use that are useful in characterizing development patterns as dense or sprawling:

(1) Density: the average number of residential units per square mile.
(2) Continuity: the degree to which land is utilized in a continuous pattern. This dimension addresses leap frog development: where areas of undeveloped land is "skipped over" leaving areas of inconsistent density and development, as opposed to land generally developed in a core outward fashion and developed with a consistent level of density.
(3) Concentration: the degree to which development is spread disproportionately over a few square miles rather than spread evenly throughout an area.
(4) Clustering: the degree which development is tightly bunched to minimize the amount of land in each square mile of developable land occupied by residential and nonresidential uses.
(5) Centrality: the degree to which development, residential and non-residential, are located close to the central business district.
(6) Nuclearity: the degree to which an urban area is composed of mononuclear or poly nuclear development.
(7) Mixed uses: the degree to which different land uses exist within the same small area and are common across the same urban area.
(8) Proximity: the degree to which different land uses are located close to each other. The mixed-use aspect is generally concerned with small areas, while proximity is concerned with the overall locations of differing land uses.
(Galster et al., 2001)

Clearly, density constitutes an important dimension of sprawl: most of the above indicators include some measure of density, or the relative compactness of various land-use patterns, as a tool for measuring sprawl. Ideally, the most valid measure of urban sprawl would be a composite index including all of the above dimensions. One group of authors selected 12 distinct dimensions of sprawl and created a measure including indicators on employment and housing land use patterns (Cutsinger, Galster, Wolman, Hanson, & Towns, 2005). Another group (Ewing et al., 2002) included the dimensions of housing mix, strength of commercial centers, and transportation accessibility, as well as residential density in their measurement of sprawl. Both studies limited their research to only a portion of the nation's MSAs, thereby reducing the possibility of broad jurisdictional comparisons.

Two studies of urban sprawl examined changes in land-use patterns among all metropolitan areas in the United States, employing composite measures for comparing growth management efforts of localities. The *USA Today* Sprawl Index (El Nasser & Overberg, 2001) compared changes from 1990 Census data with 1999 estimates in 271 MSAs in the nation. The study simply defined sprawl as the percentage of population in each MSA that lived in the Census Bureau definition of "urbanized areas," those portions of the MSA that contain 1000 or more residents per square mile. This index appears to be a valid operational measure of population density, Galster's first dimension of sprawl. However, one could also argue that this index includes other measures of sprawl because the Census Bureau states that urbanized areas must be contiguous to the core city. Therefore, continuity, the unbroken nature of land-use patterns (Galster et al., 2001), and centrality, the closeness of urban development to the city core, become part of the measure. The *USA Today* study ranked the density calculation for all 271 MSAs for both 1990 and 1999 and summed them for a composite measure of the nine-year change. Ocala, Florida had the highest index value of 536, and Laredo, Texas the lowest with 26 (El Nasser & Overberg, 2001).

Researchers at the Center on Urban and Metropolitan Policy (CUMP), an arm of the Brookings Institution, took a different approach to an operational measure of sprawl (Fulton et al., 2001). They defined density as population (estimated from the decennial census) divided by urbanized land in the MSA (classified by the National Resources Inventory's national survey of land use). Conducted every five years, this measure defines urbanized land in terms of actual land. This distinction in defining urbanized areas means that the index measures different dimensions from the *USA Today* index. The CUMP index, comparing changes in density measures between 1982 and 1997, then, includes low-density suburbs and non-contiguous urban land that would not be included in the *USA Today* measure. This index, in addition to measuring population density and continuity, like the *USA Today* index, also measures clustering and concentration since it includes the total amount of urban land in the MSA, and not simply the urbanized land adjacent to the central city. In 1997 this index, calculated in the form of a ratio, ranged from 1.23 to 12.36. The New York metropolitan area, for example, had a density ratio of 7.99. The authors of the CUMP index translated high urban densities and the maintenance of high densities to indicate better sprawl management policies (Fulton et al., 2001).

Both indices use total MSA population; however, they employ alternative definitions of urbanized land, thus measuring a combination of different dimensions of sprawl. The *USA Today* index measures sprawl in terms of its relationship to the central city, while the CUMP index measures sprawl in terms of the entire MSA. When used in combination, then, these indices include the dimensions that provide a valid measure of urban sprawl, and can be used to compare efforts in managing sprawl.

**Methodology**

The authors chose to study four core cities in moderately sized Midwestern MSAs, with populations ranging from 308,000 to 700,000: Davenport, Iowa; Omaha, Nebraska; Springfield, Missouri; and Wichita, Kansas. Since this study compares policies advocated by the Smart Growth Network, the authors selected the cities because of the range of sprawl index scores from both *USA Today* and CUMP.

Table 1 shows the ranking of the four cities according to the two measures of sprawl. The *USA Today* index shows a wide range in the efforts of the four communities in managing sprawl, with lower index values indicating better management. The CUMP index shows less variation, with higher scores reflecting

Table 1. Case-study cities ranking and results in *USA Today*'s sprawl index and the CUMP growth study.

| | \<- *USA Today* sprawl index (lower scores reflect better sprawl management) -\> | | | | | | | \<- Center on Urban & Metropolitan Policy (higher scores reflect better sprawl management) -\> | | |
|---|---|---|---|---|---|---|---|---|---|---|
| | Sprawl index score | Population, 1999 | Population in urbanized areas, 1999 (%) | National rank | Change from 1990 to 1999 (%) | Rank (1990) | Density in 1997 | Population change from 1982 to 1997 (%) | Change in urbanized land from 1982 to 1997 (%) | Change in density from 1982 to 1997 (%) |
| Davenport | 162 | 357,960 | 74.80 | 92 | −0.60 | 70 | 3.01 | −6.80 | 10.50 | −15.70 |
| Omaha | 77 | 699,385 | 85.00 | 28 | −0.20 | 49 | 4.11 | 13.20 | 25.30 | −9.70 |
| Springfield | 463 | 307,824 | 55.30 | 199 | −8.10 | 264 | 2.92 | 32.40 | 37.20 | −3.50 |
| Wichita | 300 | 549,636 | 67.70 | 129 | −3.10 | 171 | 3.02 | 15.70 | 37.40 | −15.80 |

better management. While variation exists among the four case-study cities, the indices appear to be consistent. The *USA Today* index and the CUMP index both rank Omaha first and Springfield last. Wichita and Davenport are at alternate places in the middle according to *USA Today*, but their CUMP index scores are similar.

The authors did not seek to provide a causal analysis of sprawl management, nor attempt to generalize findings to other cities; rather, the researchers sought to understand the differences among the four cities in their approach to sprawl management and determine whether the policies conformed to Smart Growth principles. Understanding has been termed a more fundamental concept for qualitative research than validity (Maxwell, 2002), and it is toward a greater understanding of the ranges of methods currently employed in selected cities that the authors strive. It is crucial in case-study analysis that the researchers recognize their own interpretation of events, documents, and policies, and understand how that affects inferences drawn from the data (Maxwell, 2002). Thus, an important question is whether the inferences drawn from the data discussed below are correct, and to what degree did the authors' inherent and cultural bias affect those inferences? With that in mind, the authors listed every document reviewed, along with the Internet address of where the documents may be located, so that readers or subsequent researchers may independently examine the data.

Analysis consisted of an inventory and examination of available planning and zoning documents as well as policy statements and initiatives for each case-study city. The authors accessed public documents via the Internet and by request, including master plans, comprehensive land-use plans, zoning and subdivision laws, and various growth and development ordinances and policies. Examining information from the planning documents, the researchers identified specific policy initiatives, programs, activities, and actions, and then compared them to Smart Growth principles.

**Case-study cities**

The following section discusses the implementation strategies of the four communities used in managing urban growth and sprawl in terms of the principles advocated by the Smart Growth Network. While the sprawl management efforts of these core communities only reflect part of the efforts of the many communities in the metropolitan statistical area, as noted previously, they nonetheless represent the policy efforts of the major or central city in the MSA that are probably exerting the greatest impact on growth and development in the moderately sized metropolitan areas.

*Springfield, Missouri*

Springfield, located in the popular Ozarks area of southern Missouri, experienced major growth during the past two decades. From 1982 to 1997, according to Table 1, the Springfield MSA population increased by 32.4%. From 1990 to 2000, the Springfield MSA population increased 23.3% to 368,374, but suburban growth exceeded central city growth by 2.7% (Henderson, 2001). Table 1 shows Springfield with a *USA Today* sprawl index score of 463 and a CUMP index score of 2.92. Both indices rank Springfield last among the case studies. Currently it ranks 199th among all MSAs, according to the *USA Today* index, but improving from 264th in 1990.

Like all cases in the study, the CUMP study showed that its population density decreased, but by the smallest margin (3.5%) from 1982 to 1997. Clearly, Springfield classifies as a sprawling community struggling with rapid growth and urbanization.

The *1999 Interim Plan* and *Executive Summary: Vision 20/20* state that Springfield desires dense, balanced, and market-oriented growth that creates alternatives to current development methods. Accordingly, the City maintains an Urban Service Area Policy, limiting city services to the capabilities of the current water treatment plants (City of Springfield, 2001b). Springfield appears to be employing many of the principles of Smart Growth, primarily through its Comprehensive Planning Office (City of Springfield, 2001c). Activity centers and targeted multi-use development within a specific geographical area, for instance, ensure mixed land uses, as do the use of zoning ordinances and the *Growth Management and Land Use Plan* (City of Springfield, 2008a). A "Key Transportation Corridors" policy and planned development also encourage mixed-use development (City of Springfield Comprehensive Planning Office, 2008a, 2008c, 2008d). The City uses Smart Growth Principles to provide housing options, create and preserve distinctive neighborhoods, and channel development toward existing communities. Finally, the *Growth Management and Land Use Plan* directs all types of development, land-use categories and locations, as well as future annexation areas. The *Comprehensive Plan* for Greene County, in which Springfield is located, addresses these same issues and uses the same implementation strategies at the county level (Greene County, 2007).

Springfield also uses a mixture of policy strategies consistent with Smart Growth principles including financial incentives, such as loans, grants, and tax credits for projects and developments that assist the city in reducing sprawl (City of Springfield, 2001a). The City uses a "neighborhood schools" concept for placement of schools intended to foster an increased neighborhood identity and influence development. The City Neighborhood Conservation Office, charged with various neighborhood focused programs and a brownfield redevelopment program, "works to assess, clean up, and facilitate the redevelopment [and] reuse of potentially contaminated properties" (City of Springfield, 2008a, 2008b; City of Springfield Comprehensive Planning Office, 2008b). Further, the City states in the *Interim Plan* that diverse housing opportunities are more likely to be realized in new neighborhoods and encourages their development through a complex public and private program called "Neighborhoods Element" (City of Springfield Comprehensive Planning Office, 2008b).

Parks, open spaces, and a greenway program address the walkable communities and open space principles of Smart Growth. Springfield maintains a major greenway system that offers 56 miles of walks and bicycle pathways, preserving drainage corridors and open spaces, as well as plans for a major downtown park (City of Springfield, 2001a, 2008b). The construction of bikeways and on-street bike lanes to encourage bicycle commuting and transportation and Key Transportation Corridors controls access and development along the city's main arterials (City of Springfield Comprehensive Planning Office, 2008c, 2008d).

Finally, Springfield encourages citizen participation on the Planning and Zoning Commission, the Board of Adjustment, and the Landmarks Board, which provides community collaboration. The "Compatible Institutional Growth" initiative requires neighborhood feedback and input prior to development or expansion (City of Springfield, 2001a).

In summary, despite its comparatively poor record of managing urban sprawl according to the indices, Springfield appears to be using a wide variety of implementation strategies. Their efforts address many of the principles of Smart Growth. This growing city has taken steps to ensure balanced development through incentives to encourage infill development and strengthening existing neighborhoods, both critical principles of Smart Growth.

*Davenport, Iowa*

Table 1 shows Davenport, Iowa, the largest city in the "Quad City" MSA, with a USA Today sprawl index score of 162 and a CUMP index score of 3.01. According to both indices, Davenport exhibits moderate levels of sprawl and continues to sprawl even though it lost population between 1990 and 1999. In fact, according to the USA Today index, Davenport dropped in the national sprawl rankings from 70th in 1990 to 92nd in 1999. While the CUMP index showed that its urbanized land increased 10.5% from 1982 to 1997, the smallest among the case studies, the city's population loss (6.8%) in that time period resulted in one of the largest decreases in density among the cases, almost 16%. Between 1990 and 2000, the Davenport–Moline–Rock Island MSA population increased only 2.1% to 370,019 while the population within Davenport declined. In other words, according to these measures, sprawling continues and increases in Davenport, despite its slow population growth.

Like many cities, Davenport employs zoning ordinances as its primary implementation strategy to meet community development goals (City of Davenport, 2000, 2005, 2007). Smart Growth principles contained in its zoning ordinances include the encouragement of compact building design and an agricultural district land-use category, encouraging green space and farmland preservation (City of Davenport, 2000). A historic preservation ordinance ensures consistent and acceptable building and redevelopment in the older sections of town and addresses the vacant and under-utilized commercial sites throughout the downtown area. A site-plan and development-plan review process and planned development districts all contribute to the Smart Growth principle encouraging predictable development decisions (City of Davenport, 2002, 2005, 2007, 2008).

Davenport also employs planned development districts for projects like the Highway Corridor Overlay District, which combine compulsory tools of zoning and regulation in combination with public information and subsidies to encourage and facilitate private development in specially designated areas or mixed-use districts in the city. Davenport also uses community development block grants to "provide decent housing and a suitable living environment, or expand economic opportunities, principally for low-and-moderate income people" (City of Davenport, 2002). In combination with block grants, the city engages private markets and voluntary organizations to help implement the *Targeted Neighborhood Program*, the *Urban Homestead Program*, and the *Housing Rehabilitation Program* that addresses three Smart Growth principles related to housing, communities, and community preservation. The *Cities Targeted Neighborhood Program* also encourages citizen input to create plans to revitalize their neighborhoods based on needs and opportunities they identify (City of Davenport, 2002).

Davenport employs a mixture of strategies to implement planning and development objectives and manage sprawl. The city takes an incremental approach to addressing other principles advocated by Smart Growth – notably housing opportunities, compact building design, and open space preservation – using mostly compulsory tools like zoning enforcement. The city apparently did not address the "walkable community" principle of Smart Growth. The American Podiatric Association labeled Davenport as the fourth worst city in which to walk (American Podiatric Medical Association, 2008).

Despite its use of several Smart Growth principles, the indices show that Davenport does not appear to be successful in managing sprawl. However, there are encouraging signs. On 7 September 2005, the city signaled a new direction in growth management by adopting *Davenport 2025: Comprehensive Plan for the City* (City of Davenport, 2005). Of particular interest to urban sprawl management and Smart Growth is the Implementation Matrix describing actions and policies needed to meet goals and objectives of the Plan. The Matrix appears to take a more active and creative approach to development issues, including more citizen involvement, and aggressive policy strategies that follow principles of Smart Growth.

## *Wichita, Kansas*

Table 1 shows Wichita with a *USA Today* sprawl index score of 300 and a CUMP index score of 3.02, ranking it third and second, respectively, among the case studies. Wichita improved its current *USA Today* ranking to 129th from 171st place in 1990. Like all the cases in the study, the CUMP study showed its population density decreasing a sizeable 15.8% from 1982 to 1997. In 2000, the Wichita MSA population increased 11.7% from 1990 to 571,166.

Wichita identifies activity centers as priority areas for multi-family and mixed-use commercial development by offering financial incentives to private developers, including beautification and amenity initiatives, land assembly and infill efforts, and location of key transit points. The City encourages the use of compact building design by allowing small-lot development in the SF-6 zoning district, a primarily single-family residential zoning district (City of Wichita, 2001). Wichita facilitates the creation of housing opportunity and choice, a Smart Growth principle, by selling vacant lots at reduced prices or at no cost at all. Wichita also uses US Department of Housing and Urban Development Community Development Block Grants, tax rebates, and fee waivers in Neighborhood Revitalization Strategy Areas and Local Investment Areas (City of Wichita, 2008a). The land-use portion of the *Comprehensive Plan* and zoning ordinances link location guidelines with each land-use category, and "are based upon factors that reflect 'good' planning practice, encourage desirable patterns of development, strive for compatibility of land use, and promote attractive urban design" (City of Wichita, 1999a, para. 33).

To encourage walkable communities, the City improved railroad right-of-ways as walking paths and offers alternative transportation including a downtown trolley/shuttle system (City of Wichita, 2001). The City's 2030 *Transit Development Plan* addresses future transportation needs, primarily personal vehicle and commuter based, and seeks improvements to local rail passenger service (Wichita–Sedgwick County Metropolitan Area, 1999).

The City encourages revitalization of older neighborhoods, another Smart Growth principle, with a specific rehabilitation code – a *Neighborhoods Revitalization Plan* – and fee waivers in Neighborhood Revitalization Areas, Local Investment Areas, and single and multi-family zoning districts (City of Wichita, 2008b). The *Historic Preservation Plan* and guidelines for development of the Old Town

Warehouse District, a distinctive, historic section of downtown Wichita, resulted in accolades for its brownfields reuse. The US Environmental Protection Agency lauded the redevelopment project in its National Awards for Smart Growth Achievement for its "effective use of public–private partnerships," and because it "capitalizes on the historic beauty of downtown Wichita" (Environmental Protection Agency, 2006). The American Planning Association nominated Old Town for one of its 2007 "10 Great Neighborhoods" awards (Wichita Area Metropolitan Planning Organization, 2008).

A "green wedge" rural zoning designation policy between Wichita and surrounding communities is employed to maintain open space and protect farmland while allowing neighboring cities to expand and maintain their unique features. The Sedgwick County's *Development Guide* employs a joint venture with the City Limits development on the southeast side of the city (City of Wichita, 1999a). The City encourages growth contiguous to current development by utilization of an Urban Service Area Policy, which defines areas that can expect city services and infrastructure to be developed or enhanced (City of Wichita, 2001).

Wichita also works to address Smart Growth principles of encouraging predictable and fair development decisions and community and stakeholder collaboration by including Planned Development Districts, *Community Unit Plans*, and the Urban Service Area Policy. The *Citizen Participation Plan* establishes the policies and procedures used to encourage citizen participation in the US Department of Housing and Urban Development five-year consolidated plan (City of Wichita, 1999b). Wichita also established District Advisory Boards and Mini-City Halls to allow citizen involvement and input on issues of concern to the community and its neighborhoods (City of Wichita, 2008a).

Wichita illustrates, however, that the utilization of a range of policy strategies embracing Smart Growth principles does not necessarily result in less urban sprawl. The city still considered the demands of the marketplace as priority in development decisions. According to the *1999 Comprehensive Plan Update*, "current, low density development/growth patterns on the edges of Wichita are desirable and justified by marketplace factors and should be encouraged into the future" (City of Wichita, 1999a, para. 5). At the same time, the plan states that the desire of the City and the Planning Commission should "encourage infill and redevelopment opportunities in central Wichita, and stabilize older residential neighborhoods throughout the City, which will require additional investment in incentives and enhanced services to these areas" (City of Wichita, 1999a, para. 5). The sprawl measures reveal Wichita's continued emphasis on fringe development and how conflicting goals may be employed in Smart Growth policy-making.

*Omaha, Nebraska*

Omaha, Nebraska ranks as the least sprawling among the four communities in this study. Table 1 shows Omaha with a *USA Today* sprawl index score of 77 and a CUMP index score of 4.11. It ranks first by both indices among the case studies in terms of levels of sprawl. In fact, *USA Today* ranks Omaha 28th among all MSAs, improving from its 49th ranking in 1990. Like all cases in the study, the CUMP study showed that its population density decreased sharply – 9.7% from 1982 to 1997 – indicating that sprawl continues in the city. In 2000 the Omaha–Council Bluffs, Nebraska–Iowa MSA population increased a respectful but not dramatic 11.8%

from 1990 to 767,041. While Omaha seems to be managing sprawl and moderate growth better than its peers in this study, sprawl remains a reality in the metropolitan area.

The Future Land Use Plan, first adopted as its Master Plan in 1993 and then modified, directs Omaha's efforts to manage urban growth. The Plan provides:

> general policies for the location of each of the City's primary land uses such as industry offices, commercial space, parks, civic facilities, and housing ... directing the pattern of land development ... to ensure that the City's limited resources are used judiciously and efficiently. (City of Omaha, 2001)

This meets the Smart Growth Principle that encourages predictable and fair development decisions.

Omaha employs a range of policy strategies to implement the principles of Smart Growth. Like most communities, Omaha relies heavily on zoning and other regulatory tools. However, city planners also use the activity center concept, a complex policy strategy that employs government subsidies and private markets to encourage private development in selected areas, leading to mixed land usage including high-density mixed use and convenience mixed use.

The City also encourages compact building design in the form of developer fees for access to city water and sewer services and as an encouragement for higher density development. The fees facilitate contiguous higher density development by making it more economical for developers to build more homes per site, thus creating more walkable communities. The city also encourages higher density development by offering density bonuses and incentives to developers who build zero-lot-line housing subdivisions.

The Sanitary and Improvement District (SID), provided by state statutes, is a unique tool for development. It enables developers to create temporary special districts to finance large-scale developments by issuing government bonds, repaid by future homeowners in the development. Market forces ultimately determine the success of the development project. SIDs must meet city planning and zoning standards if they are within three miles of Omaha's city limits and in the same county. SIDs may provide housing opportunities and choices, sometimes resulting in distinctive communities and mixed land uses (Blair, 2001), all aspects of Smart Growth. However, they may encourage sprawl in the absence of a strong regional plan and zoning ordinances and may complicate Omaha's efforts to curb sprawl by providing capital to develop in the periphery of the urbanized area. Future research should determine the effect of SIDs on sprawl.

The *Future Land Use Plan* states that new development, including that of SIDs within the county, must "encourage pedestrian, mass transit and alternative modes of transportation" (City of Omaha, 2001). Redevelopment of railroad right-of-ways as bicycle and pedestrian greenways meets the Smart Growth goals to create walkable communities and provide alternative transportation choices. Defined "gateway areas" offer distinctive and attractive entrances into the city and the *Land Use Concept Plan* includes consistent design and construction standards to ensure an attractive community (City of Omaha, 2001). In 2007, a public–private partnership called Omaha By Design[2] focused on civic, neighborhood and environmental improvement and resulted in a major revision of the city's urban design element of the *Master Plan*, with efforts in other policy areas related to urban development ongoing. The Omaha by Design plan includes neighborhood, civic, and green components as well as land-use and transportation elements.

To strengthen development within existing neighborhoods, Omaha encourages contiguous development, the use of grants for neighborhood conservation, improvement plans, and historic preservation. The City also offers various incentives for redevelopment of existing areas, both residential and commercial. Projects such as the redevelopment of the old Livestock Exchange building and stockyards – which is being repurposed into a commercial area and a proposed assisted living facility – provide examples of the types of redevelopment undertaken by Omaha in core and historic areas of town.

In comparison with the other cases studied, Omaha appears to be managing urban sprawl in a relatively effective manner, using a wider variety of policy strategies. However, perhaps its most valuable tool is a liberal annexation law that provides a clear, compulsory mechanism to manage growth and development in the city's periphery within the county (Blair, 2001).

**Findings and discussion**

Because of the role of sprawl in exacerbating regional and urban inequities, this study questioned the role of the Smart Growth Network in providing guidance to cities in the management of urban sprawl. In particular, what factors account for variation in planning and policy approaches? Do policy recommendations espoused by the Smart Growth Network help address urban sprawl? Is adherence to a greater number of Smart Growth principles associated with higher sprawl management rankings? Most importantly, do the advocates of growth management provide policy guidance and strategies to better control urban sprawl?

The authors submit a number of general summary statements resulting from case-study analysis. Most importantly, the case studies communities fail to reduce sprawl regardless of the level of their use of Smart Growth principles. Densities continue to decrease. Intuitively, the wide use of a variety of Smart Growth principles should reduce urban sprawl, but not according to the indices of the case studies. The authors suggest that the Smart Growth Network instead emphasizes a holistic policy approach to sprawl management rather than emphasizing a set of individual policy principles. Nonetheless, the case studies do provide insight on the relationship between Smart Growth principles and the management of sprawl.

First, while the USA Today and CUMP sprawl indices (Table 1) show apparent differences in how well cities manage sprawl, analysis of planning and development documents from the communities in the case studies does not clearly show that there are major differences in the variety of policy strategies utilized. This study revealed that the case-study communities employed a range of policies, and that most policies generally followed principles of Smart Growth. Levels of adherence to Smart Growth Principles, then, at least according to these case studies, do not explain differences among the communities in terms of the ranking of sprawl management indices. As the case-study analysis indicates, each city incorporated a number of policies advocated by the Smart Growth Network to control urban sprawl. For example, while Omaha, according to the indices, appears to be managing sprawl better than the other cities in the study, it did not employ substantially more principles of Smart Growth than Springfield, which sprawled the most.

A second summary statement offered by the authors suggests that policy approaches to combating urban sprawl involve more than simply summing the number of principles of Smart Growth that the cities implement. Subtle differences among the types of policies and implementation strategies may offer an explanation. The authors note that the level of adherence to market conditions and forces that favor suburban development in some locales and mixed-use development in other cities may explain some cities' proclivity to sprawl (e.g. Wichita's emphasis on developing single-family homes in the city's periphery).

While case-study data show some differences in the number of Smart Growth principles the cities followed, the variation among the communities in the types of overall policy strategies employed and emphasized may offer some insight. Clearly, the four case-study communities took different overall implementation approaches in terms of managing sprawl. The authors offer Table 2 to provide a typology for the approaches.

Traditional approaches to growth management focus on compulsory, regulatory policy tools, like planning and zoning, and follow fewer Smart Growth principles. Davenport and Springfield appear to follow this method, not by using more compulsory policy tools than other cities, but by focusing their strategies and efforts in top-down approaches. A government-centered approach emphasizes traditional compulsory government strategies and tools, yet adopts more Smart Growth principles than a traditional approach. Alternatively, a market-based approach employs more mixed, or voluntary, policy tools like private markets and voluntary organizations, yet follows a relatively small number of Smart Growth principles. Wichita appears to take this approach. In the public–private or partnership approach, government and business collaborate in development, especially in the suburban fringe, as in the case study. Because of the Omaha By Design effort described in the case study, Omaha provides an example of this type of approach.

In addition to the providing a detailed look at the relationship between sprawl management strategies and the number of Smart Growth principles adopted, case-study analysis reveals other observations on urban sprawl management. First, cities with a higher level of commitment to planning (e.g. more ongoing and participatory planning) and which cite growth as a key city issue or a core community value seem to employ a greater number and variety of policy strategies that address the Smart Growth principles and growth management. Second, long-range vision statements like Springfield's *Vision 20/20* appear to provide a platform for the city to analyze future growth and sprawl management as an over-arching value, rather than focusing on single issues or problems. Third, while the characteristics of the implementing agencies were similar, the levels of internalization by government agencies of various growth management philosophies varied. For example, Omaha drew information from a *Master Plan* and *Future Land Use Plan* created over a decade ago. Alternately, Davenport appears to have just begun to address comprehensive issues like park planning and consensus on a community-wide

Table 2. Approaches to sprawl management.

| Policy strategies utilized | Smart growth principles employed | |
| --- | --- | --- |
|  | Few | Many |
| Compulsory/mixed | Traditional | Government-centered |
| Mixed/voluntary | Market-based | Public–private partnership |

plan. Finally, inter-organizational communication and enforcement activities were not readily apparent from the case studies. Cities are often part of a larger metropolitan statistical area and within that MSA, regional planning authorities may exist. Regional collaboration is one factor that could assist each of these cities in meeting future growth effectively. Each of the cities studied did not manage growth and urban sprawl in isolation; the role of state government, with its own polices and priorities should be remembered.

Sprawl has a profound effect on regional equity concerns. When scarce development resources are directed to the fringes of a community, the result is often a disinvestment of core urban communities. Those who can afford to move to newer neighborhoods will leave the inner city to the poor and disadvantaged. This has an impact on social equity since tax revenues, supporting social services for those least able to pay for them, generated by the mobile middle and upper classes depart from the city with fleeing population. Local government policy-makers and administrators need to find ways to manage urban sprawl, and, as seen in these four case-study cities, approaches can be varied, involving multiple agents, and targeting distinct policy communities.

What key lessons do these four case-study cities provide? First, sprawl management requires a vision for a city for its future development. To become effective, the vision should developed by stakeholders and incorporated into planning documents such as the zoning ordinances, master plans, comprehensive plans, and future land-use plans. Second, growth management should be an overriding philosophy, linking land use and transportation planning to development and rehabilitation decisions made daily in departments, city councils, and planning commissions. Finally, successful growth management depends on implementation of a broad variety of policy tools and strategies from voluntary and mixed level tools through compulsory tools. Policy strategies that consider and utilize private-sector markets play an important role in sprawl management. As shown by the case studies, a city cannot depend on zoning and coercion alone to control sprawl.

## Acknowledgements

An earlier version of this paper was presented by Robert Blair and Elaine Placido at a regional conference of the American Society for Public Administration. The authors thank Dick Esseks and Jerry Deichert for their assistance with methodological issues on earlier drafts.

## Notes

1. See http://www.smartgrowth.org.
2. See http://www.omahabydesign.org.

## References

Allen, J.T. (1999, September 6). Sprawl, from here to eternity. *U.S. News and World Report* (pp. 22–25).
American Podiatric Medical Association. (2008). *Best (and worst) walking cities in America*. Retrieved from http://www.apma.org/s_apma/bin.asp?CID=251&DID=22708&DOC=FILE.PDF.
Bartle, J., & Wellman, G. (2010). *Sustainability makes dollars and sense*. Omaha, NE: Omaha by Design.

Black, T.J., & Curtis, R. (1993). *The local fiscal effects of growth and commercial development over time*. Washington, DC: Urban Land Institute.

Blair, R.F. (2001). Managing urban growth: Can the policy tools approach improve effectiveness? *Public Works Management and Policy, 6*(2), 102–113.

Boschken, H.L. (2002). *Social class, politics, and urban markets: The makings of bias in policy outcomes*. Stanford, CA: Stanford University Press.

Burchell, R.W. (1998). *Cost of sprawl revisited: The evidence of sprawl's negative and positive impacts*. Washington, DC: National Transportation Research Board and National Research Council.

Ciscel, D.H. (2001). The economics of urban sprawl: Inefficiency as a core feature of metropolitan growth. *Journal of Economic Issues, 35*(2), 405–413.

City of Davenport. (2000). *Code of the City of Davenport Iowa*. Avon, NJ: Coded Systems Corporation. Retrieved from http://www.davenportiowa.org

City of Davenport. (2002). *Urban Homestead Program, Targeted Neighborhood Program, Housing Rehabilitation Program, Community Development Block Grant Administration*. Community & Economic Development Home Page. Retrieved March 29, 2002, from http://www.davenportiowa.org

City of Davenport. (2005). *Planning and zoning – Davenport 2025: Comprehensive plan for the city*. Community & Economic Development Home Page. Retrieved from http://www.davenportiowa.org

City of Davenport. (2007). *Davenport 2025: Comprehensive plan and recommendations*. Retrieved from http://www.davenportiowa.org

City of Davenport. (2008). *Design center feedback forum*. Retrieved from http://www.davenportiowa.org/department/division.asp?fDD = 11–159

City of Omaha. (2001). *Future land use plan*. Retrieved from www.ci.omaha.ne.us/planning/landuse.3htm

City of Springfield. (2001a). *Planning and development*. Retrieved from www.ci.springfield.mo.us/egov/planning_development/index.html

City of Springfield. (2001b). *Vision 20/20, Interim plan and executive summary*. Retrieved from www.ci.springfield.mo.us/community/vision20–20/index.html

City of Springfield. (2008a). *City of Springfield brownfields program*. Retrieved from http://www.ci.springfield.mo.us/egov/planning_development/econ_dev/brownfields/index.html

City of Springfield. (2008b). *Comprehensive planning office*. Retrieved from http://www.ci.springfield.mo.us/egov/planning_development/plan_services/index.html

City of Springfield Comprehensive Planning Office. (2008a). *Growth management and land use plan*. Retrieved from http://www.ci.springfield.mo.us/egov/planning_development/plan_services/pdfs/comp_plan/growth.pdf

City of Springfield Comprehensive Planning Office. (2008b). *Neighborhoods element*. Retrieved from http://www.ci.springfield.mo.us/egov/planning_development/plan_services/pdfs/

City of Springfield Comprehensive Planning Office. (2008c). *Planning and zoning commission*. Retrieved from http://www.ci.springfield.mo.us/egov/boards/plan_zon/index.html/comp_plan/neighborhoods.pdf

City of Springfield Comprehensive Planning Office. (2008d). *Southeast Springfield development study*. Retrieved from http://www.ci.springfield.mo.us/egov/planning_development/se_dev_study/se_dev_study.pdf

City of Wichita. (1999a) *Comprehensive plan: Preparing for Change: Wichita land use and Sedgwick County development guides, Wichita residential area enhancement area strategy, and transportation plan update*. Retrieved from http://www.wichitagov.org

City of Wichita. (1999b). *Wichita ... Positioned for the next century, City of Wichita Consolidated Plan 2000–2004*. Retrieved from http://www.wichitagov.org

City of Wichita. (2001). *Wichita land use guide*. Retrieved from http://www.wichitagov.org/NR/rdonlyres/6B98DEC0-E245-4369-92B8-5A670573BADA/0/Wichita_Land_Use_Guide_16d.pdf

City of Wichita. (2008a). *History of planning in Wichita–Sedgwick County*. Retrieved from http://www.wichitagov.org/CityOffices/Planning/mapd_history.htm

City of Wichita. (2008b). *Neighborhood revitalization plans*. Retrieved from http://www.wichitagov.org/CityOffices/Planning/AP/NR/

Cutsinger, J., Galster, G., Wolman H., Hanson R., & Towns, D. (2005). Verifying the multidimensional nature of metropolitan land use: Advancing the understanding and measurement of sprawl. *Journal of Urban Affairs, 27*(3), 235–259.

Danielsen, K.A., Lang, R.E., & Fulton, W. (1998). What does smart growth mean for housing? *Housing Facts & Findings, 1*(3), 11–15.

Downs, A. (1999). Some realities about sprawl and urban decline. *Housing Policy Debate, 10,* 955–974.

El Nasser, H., & Overberg, P. (2001, February 22). What you don't know about sprawl: Controlling development a big concern, but analysis has unexpected findings. *USA Today.* Retrieved from http://pqasb.pqarchiver.com/USAToday/

Environmental Protection Agency. (2006). *2006 national award for smart growth achievement.* Retrieved from http://www.epa.gov/smartgrowth/awards/sg_awards_publication_2006.htm#built_projects

Ewing, R., Pendall, R., & Chen, D. (2002). *Measuring sprawl and its impact.* Washington, DC: Smart Growth America.

Fulton, W., Pendall, R., Nguyen, M., & Harrison, A. (2001). *Who sprawls most? How growth patterns differ across the U.S.* Washington, DC: The Brookings Institute, Center on Urban and Metropolitan Policy.

Galster, G., Hanson, R., Ratcliffe, M.R., Wolman, H., Coleman, S., & Freihage, J. (2001). Wrestling sprawl to the ground. *Housing Policy Debate, 12*(4), 681–717.

Gordon, P., & Richardson, H. (2001). The sprawl debate: Let markets plan. *Publius, 31*(3), 131–149.

Greene County. (2007). *Proposed comprehensive plan.* Retrieved from http://www.greenecountymo.org/web/About/comprehensive_plan.php

Harvey, D. (2009). *Social justice and the city.* Athens, GA: The University of Georgia Press.

Henderson, C.B. (2001). *Suburbs growing faster in Fed's eighth district.* The Federal Reserve Bank of Saint Louis. Retrieved from http://www.stlouisfed.org/news/releases/2001/10_11_01_a.html

Howlett, M., & Ramesh, M. (1995). *Studying public policy: Policy cycles and policy subsystems.* Oxford, UK: Oxford University Press.

Katz, B., & Bradley, J. (1999, December). Divided we sprawl. *The Atlantic Monthly.* Retrieved from http://www.theatlantic.com/issues/99dec/9912katz.htm

Logan, J.R., & Molotch, H.L. (1987). *Urban fortunes: The political economy of place.* Los Angeles, CA: University of California Press.

Maxwell, J.A. (2002). Understanding and validity in qualitative research. In A.M. Huberman & M.B. Miles (Eds.), *The qualitative researcher's companion* (pp. 37–64). Thousand Oaks, CA: Sage Publications.

Palen, J.J. (2008). *The urban world* (8th ed.). Boulder, CO: Paradigm Publishers.

Porter, D.R. (1997). *Managing growth in America's communities.* In cooperation with members of The Growth Management Institute. Washington, DC: Island Press.

Powell, M.W. (2000, August 17). Let liberty, sense shape urban growth. *Omaha World Herald,* 27.

Rusk, D. (2000). Growth management: The core regional issue. In B. Katz (Ed.), *Reflections on regionalism* (pp. 78–1060). Washington, DC: Brookings Institute.

Sabatier, P.A., & Jenkins-Smith, H.C. (1999). The advocacy coalition framework: An assessment. In P.Sabatier (Ed.), *Theories of the policy process* (pp. 117–168). Boulder, CO: Westview Press.

Smart Growth Network. (2010). *Principles of smart growth.* Retrieved from http://www.smartgrowth.org/about/principles/default.asp

Stoel, T.B. (1999). Reigning in urban sprawl. *Environment, 41*(4), 6–17.

Squires, G.D. (Ed.). (2002). *Urban sprawl: Causes, consequences & policy responses.* Washington, DC: The Urban Institute Press.

Wichita Area Metropolitan Planning Organization. (2008). *Metro planning news.* Retrieved from http://www.wichitagov.org/NR/rdonlyres/89097A38-4EF1-48E1-826F-00651BEE2A37/0/metroplnnewsspring08.pdf

Wichita–Sedgwick County Metropolitan Area. (1999). *2030 Transportation plan, 1999 update.* Retrieved from http://www.wichita.gov/NR/rdonlyres/7E166218-37EE-4862-9E47-692A8DD4ED5F/0/1999UpddatetotheZ030TransporPlan.pdf

Williamson, T., Imbroscio, D., & Alperovitz, G. (2005). The challenge of urban sprawl. In N.Kleniewski (Ed.), *Cities and Society* (pp. 303–329). Maldin, MA: Blackwell Publishing.

# Regional equity through community development planning: the Metro Detroit Regional Investment Initiative

Jane Morgan[a] and Sujata Shetty[b]

[a]*JFM Consulting Group, USA;* [b]*Department of Geography and Planning, University of Toledo, USA*

> Beginning in late 2003, the Detroit Local Initiatives Support Corporation, with Ford Foundation funding, began a yearlong community-based process to arrive at a conceptual idea of what regional equity means in the Detroit region. This process, called the Metro Detroit Regional Investment Initiative (MDRII), resulted in the formation of several coalitions of Detroit community groups and the local governments of some of the city's inner-ring suburbs. Three cross-border coalitions were funded and have embarked on a pilot project that seeks to *implement* the idea of regional equity. These three coalitions are currently working both to build relationships with each other and to work on joint community development projects. For those familiar with the Detroit of metro region and its history of contentious city–suburb relations, this collaboration is unprecedented. This paper studies the MDRII to examine the process and outcomes so far. Methods used include surveys, focus groups, and long interviews with members of the participating communities and governments. A critical examination of the process provides the opportunity to link regional equity to community development and draw specific lessons for practice.

## Introduction

The Detroit metropolitan region has had a long history of racial segregation, unequal development, and contentious city–suburb relationships. The area boasts little regional cooperation, and in a trend that has accelerated as the region has experienced economic decline, Detroit has been joined by some of its inner-ring suburbs in experiencing increasing rates of unemployment, lower average incomes, declining housing stock, and related problems. This is consistent with the findings in many other inner-ring suburbs in the mid-west (Puentes and Warren, 2006).

In 2004, the Ford Foundation was looking to fund pilot projects that would address issues related to urban sprawl and concurrent spatial inequities. The State of Michigan was beginning to pay attention to sprawl and, in June 2004, announced a "Cool Cities" initiative, promoted as a policy to reinvest in Michigan's cities as a way to address sprawl, encourage economic development, and reverse the state's "brain drain". Detroit Local Initiatives Support Corporation (LISC) was also beginning to see that small-scale community development projects were not having much impact on the community as a whole, and that a broader approach was necessary. There appeared to be a convergence of interest in combating sprawl.

In late 2003, Detroit LISC embarked on a 3-year pilot project that aimed to address in some meaningful way the consequences of urban sprawl, and its impacts on Detroit and adjacent inner-ring suburban neighbors. Regional equity, an approach that argues that urban poverty and suburban sprawl are linked and that planning should be undertaken at the metropolitan level (Center for Justice, Community and Tolerance, 2006; PolicyLink, 2003), was seen as a model that could help frame this work in the Detroit metro region. This article addresses two specific questions:

- How was "regional equity" conceptualized and implemented in Detroit?
- What lessons about regional equity can we draw for community development planning?

We use the experience in Detroit to argue that contrary to the conventional understanding of regional planning as large-scale undertakings (a regional environmental plan or a regional transportation plan, for example), small-scale cross-jurisdictional community development collaborations, incrementally, also constitute regional planning. We also argue that the cross-jurisdictional nature of these collaborations does not automatically result in regional equity, even when that is the overall goal. Issues of race and social equity have to be addressed directly, parallel to designing and implementing community development planning projects that aim to achieve regional equity.

## Framing regional equity in Michigan and Detroit

Orfield and Luce (2003) contend that Michigan's growth patterns have resulted in at least three categories of consequences: sprawl, fiscal inequities between local governments, and social separation.

### *Sprawl*

Between 1970 and 2000, the amount of developed land in Michigan increased about 10 times faster than the population (Orfield and Luce, 2003). Concurrent with trends toward sprawl during 1970–2000, there was a decline in population in Detroit and inner-ring suburbs, while outer suburbs increased in population.

This sprawl had given rise to a very wide range of communities in the region. Orfield and Luce (2003) divide them into seven categories: central cities, stressed suburbs, at-risk established suburbs, at-risk low-density suburbs, bedroom/developing suburbs, low-stress suburbs, and industrial towns. Central cities are highly stressed compared to other communities in the region. Stressed suburbs, which include inner-ring suburbs, face declining populations or slow growth, aging infrastructure, low median incomes, and schools with high rates of student poverty. Continuing the pattern inherent in the location of these communities, those communities with the highest median income are located away from the central city. These communities have very limited housing options, keeping out most low- and middle-income workers, thereby restricting their access to good public services.

Uneven fiscal development has been another consequence of Michigan's growth pattern. Orfield and Luce (2003) also found that local governments in Michigan with a large tax base have three to eight times more revenue raising capacity than those governments with the lowest tax base. This has direct implications for the services that local governments can provide. Public schools in central cities like Detroit, Flint and Saginaw are being closed because of the declining population, while other communities, such as Ann Arbor and Saline, have recently invested in very expensive new school buildings.

Michigan makes it very difficult for communities to annex surrounding areas, making them "inelastic" (Rusk, 1993), but easy for a community to incorporate itself. Michigan is also very dependent on local tax bases to provide public services. This leads to a highly fragmented administrative system where communities compete to increase their tax base, greatly limiting the incentive to think regionally and work cooperatively.

## *Segregation*

According to the data from the 2000 census, analyzed by the Lewis Mumford Center at the University at Albany, SUNY (n.d.), Detroit is the most segregated metropolitan region in the country, with an index of dissimilarity of 84.7. (A score of 100 indicates complete segregation.) Within the region, race and poverty are highly correlated. In 2001, 70% of elementary school students in Detroit were eligible for free school lunches. This compares to 60% in stressed communities and 11% in low-stress communities. Median income in Detroit was $29,526, compared to $37,806 in stressed communities and $84,866 in low-stress communities. Between 1995 and 2000, household growth was 10% in low-stress communities, unchanged in stressed communities; the number of households declined by 8% in Detroit (Orfield and Luce, 2003).

## *Regional equity*

Many authors (Orfield, 2002) have argued that metropolitan-level regional cooperation is important if inequities are to be addressed. Orfield (2002), for example, has shown a relationship between decline in the central city and flourishing outer-ring suburbs, arguing that central city residents are subsidizing the development of newer suburbs. But while the multiplicity of local jurisdictions is an impediment to regional cooperation, in Detroit, there have been other factors that have played a role as well.

The region's racial history is one factor. The region has had at least five decades of dramatic conflict over access to housing in the suburbs for African Americans and efforts by suburban jurisdictions to separate themselves from the central city (Simmons, 2002).

The tensions of racial segregation and economic segregation have been exacerbated by the extremely severe economic troubles in the state. Residents of metro Detroit are closely tied to the fortunes of the auto industry and are feeling the harsh impact of its dramatic decline. For many decades, car factories had been a source of stable, relatively well-paying jobs, positions which have now mostly disappeared.

A series on racial segregation ran in the Detroit News in 2002, and asked if metro Detroiters were choosing to live amicably, but apart, by race. Based on 2000 census data, Livonia, a suburb of Detroit, was the whitest city of more than 100,000 in the US, while Detroit had the second-largest black majority in the country. Only 6% of metro Detroit residents lived in neighborhoods that remotely resemble the racial makeup of the community as a whole. Yet, the paper reported that the vast majority of residents they spoke to did not consider their own communities segregated (French, 2002).

Politicians have not paid particular attention to segregation either. To quote from the article (French, 2002):

> "Few community leaders consider segregation a problem today, nor are they eager to question why blacks and whites live more separately in Metro Detroit than anywhere else. Segregated housing is frequently a taboo topic among politicians, many of whom either say segregation doesn't exist, or it no longer has a negative impact."

It is clear then that metro Detroit is dealing urban sprawl, fiscal inequity, segregation, and limited regional cooperation, all of which, in turn, shape people's access to resources and opportunities based on their location. Given their specific spatial distribution, these challenges are place-based. But given their basis in individual experience, responses to these challenges have to be people-based as well. Regional equity provides a theoretical framework that allows both to be addressed simultaneously. As Glover-Blackwell and Fox (2004) contend, regional equity has been informed by, among other things, the smart growth movement; the civil rights movement, which offers a racial perspective to analyze growth patterns; neighborhood revitalization and community development efforts which suggest that "place matters" and that physical revitalization of distressed communities to improve outcomes for residents. The community building movement, they suggest, provides a framework that leads regional equity toward "holistic, comprehensive approaches to the needs of low-income communities, underscoring the connection between 'people' and 'place' based strategies" (Glover-Blackwell and Fox, 2004, p. 4).

## Methodology

The authors have been involved with the Metro Detroit Regional Investment Initiative (MDRII) since its inception, initially as facilitators of a community-based planning process that helped to clarify what a regional equity project would look like in metro Detroit. This part of the project involved individual interviews and focus groups.

For the ongoing evaluation of the project, we have continued to use a community-based, participatory model. In addition to feedback from LISC, we have an evaluation advisory group comprising participants in the project. These participants have provided feedback on our survey and focus group instruments, as well as met periodically for data interpretation sessions. We used two annual surveys – one to gather data on the project in general and the second to focus on the issues of collaboration. We also conducted individual interviews with participants and LISC staff and were participant observers at several meetings of the three collaboratives. Results for this paper derive from 35 surveys, 1 focus group, and 21 individual interviews.

## The case: the Metro Detroit Regional Investment Initiative

In response to a request from the Ford Foundation, in 2004, Detroit LISC embarked on a process that aimed to address in some meaningful way the consequences of urban sprawl and its impact on Detroit and adjacent *inner-ring* suburban neighbors.

The question posed to potential partners in the planning process was: how would they provide comprehensive, equitable resources and opportunities for residents while addressing one or more issues negatively affecting adjacent but cross-jurisdictional neighborhoods? The only nonnegotiable items LISC set down for residents, community-based organizations and municipalities were that any proposed strategy be inclusive; promote and encourage the creation of diverse communities; and encourage physical revitalization and/or development in the "edge" communities.

### *Planning process*

The first step was to convene a diverse group of stakeholders who could provide important skills, experience, and knowledge to the regional equity planning design. These stakeholders included: Michigan and National LISC programs, the local foundation community, academic institutions, the financial and intermediary community, place-based and community-based nonprofit organizations, diversity and race relations experts, regional organizations, city, county and state government.

The stakeholders shaped a multisession planning process that would bring together as many diverse and interested parties as possible, developed criteria for what a regional equity project would look like, recommended that it be competitive, and provided resources to flesh out concepts prior to making final awards. These stakeholders also recommended that the collaborating parties develop projects in response to their own cross-jurisdictional neighborhood needs. They identified the racial divide as one of the biggest barriers to regional cooperation and urged that MDRII take this on specifically.

The resulting process included three planning sessions open to community-based organizations, block clubs, community development organizations, local government, businesses, academia, and almost any group interested in putting forth the effort to make a more cooperative regional landscape. Some of the outcomes included: development of a steering committee to guide the program; criteria to be implemented by the work plans; and how selection of groups could occur.

LISC staff and MDRII steering committee members developed and finalized the "request for proposal" (RFP) and selection criteria for the program. At a meeting in early November 2004, the RFP was presented to approximately 125 people representing city and suburban municipalities, nonprofit agencies, and community development corporations. Detroit LISC staff, Michigan Suburbs Alliance (MSA), and volunteer planning firms attended meetings and provided feedback to the groups as they formulated their concept papers in response to the RFP.

### *Site selection*

In mid-December 2004, 12 concept papers were submitted for consideration. Seven selected partnerships were awarded a $25,000 planning grant for the 4-month period to develop the comprehensive 3-year plan due in June 2005. Following this, three of the groups received full funding, while the remaining four groups could receive partial funding.

*Structuring the process*

LISC developed a 10–15 member Executive Steering Committee that would report to the Detroit LISC Local Advisory Committee. LISC hired staff specifically for this project, who, among other tasks, developed grant guidelines that were guided by the criteria recommended by the stakeholders. Criteria included four primary goal areas that would have to be equitably addressed: policy, community building, physical revitalization, and neighborhood revitalization.

The MDRII marshaled additional resources to provide the seven groups with the expertise they would need to develop their work plans during the 4-month planning period and continued support for the three selected groups.

- The MSA provided guidance and assistance to the seven partnerships that received the planning grant. Then, MSA assisted the final groups in developing relationships with their suburban partners and provided guidance as the groups were developing and implementing their 3-year strategies.
- The Michigan Land Use Institute also played an integral role in the organization of the MDRII Speakers Series, by helping in identifying topics, attracting speakers, handling logistical concerns, and providing additional expertise as needed.
- Michigan Roundtable on Diversity and Inclusion (MRDI) was the driving force behind the Race and Cultural Relations Training. During the planning grant phase, each group had members attend 2.5 days of training. MRDI helped the three selected collaborative groups incorporate diversity into their thinking and help create, modify, or implement their race and cultural strategies.
- New Detroit addresses race relations by positively impacting issues and policies that ensure economic and social equity. New Detroit assisted Detroit LISC and the Executive Steering Committee to develop outcomes for the program around race strategies.

*The three sites*

*Detroit–Grosse Pointe Collaborative (DGPC)*

The DGPC is composed of several Detroit organizations that are longstanding members of the community and have a successful track record of programming and development and the City of Grosse Pointe Park. This area has arguably the most dramatic contrast of the three collaborative groups. Detroit's population is 7% white and 89% black. The median income is $16,500, the poverty rate hovers around 46%, and the median home value is $28,300. Grosse Pointe Park, literally across the street from Detroit, is 91% white and 3% black. The median income is $80,500, the poverty rate is around 4%, and the median home value is $331,200.

Since the beginning of the program, people were skeptical that the DGPC would be successful in engaging the leadership and residents of Grosse Pointe Park. DGPC has proven otherwise, which is exemplified in the work that they are doing to break down real and perceived barriers to regional cooperation. DGPC has really meshed into a unified collaborative that is working for the betterment of the area.

Utilizing the MDRII as a platform, these partners were able to garner the participation of Grosse Pointe Park. Each work plan component included community organizing: business organizing/community development; neighborhood organizing/housing development; and youth and recreation. This strategic focus led to hiring a community organizer on staff to lead and coordinate activities and continually engage residents.

The DGPC activities focused on developing commercial space, facade improvement along a commercial street, and a cross-border business association. Within the target commercial corridors, the DGPC has completed 10 facade improvements for local businesses, improved the local business network through the cross-border neighborhood association, and is beginning to organize business improvement districts and making progress on major streetscape improvements. The DGPC has focused on building community relations through beautification projects, cross-border neighborhood associations, and holiday parties to bring together youth from Detroit and Grosse Pointe.

A signature physical development project for the DGPC is the Alter Road Transformation (ART). ART will develop a master plan to "transform" Alter Road from its current blighted state to a more welcoming border between Detroit and Grosse Pointe. For housing development, LISC, through MDRII, provided financing to an area community development corporation (CDC) for 10 new single-family for-sale homes to be built on in-fill lots located on a single, highly visible block near the targeted commercial corridor.

Each summer DGPC has sponsored MOSIAC, an internationally acclaimed professional performing art training program which achieves youth development through the arts. Over 180 youth have participated in the program, which began as a drama program and expanded to also include dance and vocal performance. The program boasts a 50/50 split of participants from Detroit and Grosse Pointe. The DGPC joined forces with Wayne County Community College to provide a service learning course for 15–20 junior and seniors from Detroit and Grosse Pointe High Schools. Race relations and social inequity are the foundation of the course syllabus.

*Van Dyke/8 Mile Gateway Collaborative (V8-Gateway)*

V8-Gateway comprises Detroit organizations and two neighboring suburbs: Center Line and Warren. Eight Mile Road is the metaphor that symbolizes metro Detroit's status as the nation's most segregated urban–suburban region. Eight Mile Road is the northern border of Detroit in this area. There is a long history of racial stereotyping and prejudice between Detroit and its northern suburban neighbors. The demographics of the areas here are remarkably similar with regard to income and levels of education. V8-Gatetway's focus is the commercial revitalization of Van Dyke Avenue, which cuts through all three communities.

The members of the Gateway have made strides to bridge the divide between Detroit and Warren and Center Line. The components of the V8-Gateway strategy focus on commercial corridor improvement, youth development, and beautification. As a result of these activities, the organizations and residents have developed a shared community vision and are working together to benefit the entire area.

In the first year of the program, the members of the Gateway came together to develop one set of design guidelines for facade improvement along Van Dyke Avenue. Each of the three areas had their own set of guidelines, and the collaborative realized that these could be more effective if merged into one. These guidelines have been accepted and are now utilized by each of the municipalities in the collaborative. When the City of Warren receives plans for new facades or development along commercial corridors, they consult with the members of the Gateway to make sure what they approve is consistent with the plans of the Gateway. In addition, the city of Warren also extended their Tax Increment Financing Authority boundaries to 8 Mile Road, so that its resources could be utilized near the Detroit border.

Michigan State University Extension, a Gateway partner, has extended two programs, Practical Home and Garden and Curb Appeal for Business, to residents and businesses in Detroit. These programs offer courses on outdoor maintenance and beautification, along with a $300 Lowe's gift card to make minor home repairs or to buy supplies for yard/curb appeal. The Gateway also hosts two youth programs, *Outstanding Neighborhood Enterprise (O.N.E. Youth)*, which brings high school age youth from Detroit and the neighboring suburbs together to attack the challenging issues that lead to neighborhood deterioration and decline, and *Youth Power*, which focuses on youth under the age of 14 and promotes responsibility and self-esteem. Youth participate in conflict resolution and violence prevention activities addressing race and socioeconomic division between communities bordering 8 Mile Road.

*Fort/Visger Collaborative*

In contrast to the other two collaborative groups, Fort/Visger has experienced changes within the members of the collaborative since its application to be a part of the MDRII in 2004. Current partners are Detroit community organizations and the cities of Ecorse, Lincoln Park, and River Rouge. Although located in very close proximity, these communities had little prior history of working together. Through a concert series, farmers' market and cleaning and greening activities, Fort/Visger has been successful in blurring the lines between the cities and erasing previous perceptions that had hindered collaboration.

The steering committee of Fort/Visger identified the need for a multi-jurisdictional CDC. A formal board is in place for the CDC and the 501(c)(3) application has been submitted. The need for affordable housing in the area was also a priority. In order to determine the best areas for redevelopment, the collaborative conducted a feasibility study for the development of 20–30 for-sale homes. The study recommended converting up to 28 lots into new in-fill affordable for-sale housing units; working with existing homeowners to repair or rehabilitate existing homes. Since the study was completed, market conditions and other factors have necessitated less emphasis on for-sale housing and more emphasis on establishing the repair/rehab program.

**Results**

Below are the highlights of the results, based on surveys, focus group, and interviews. These highlights are categorized by how the participants perceive the results – as strengths, weaknesses, or as being mixed. We have also categorized the results based on the method of data collection. The surveys provide a broad picture, while the interviews and focus groups provide more nuance and add detail on complex questions.

*Survey results*

When asked what their organization hoped to achieve as an MDRII stakeholder, the largest number of responses referred to the idea of a region, and achieving social and economic equity in that region. For example,

- "... to create a cohesive and equitable region that provides revitalization and social equity through outreach and racially diverse interaction."
- "To work together with the City of Detroit and inner-ring suburbs to address common social equity issues."
- "... to provide social equity activities that continue to break down the physical and social barriers between Detroit and the Grosse Pointes."

Also important was the idea of the sustainability of the work of MDRII, which respondents linked to collaboration. Among the comments:

- "... creation of a structure by which Grosse Pointe Park and Detroit neighbors can work together on common projects/and problems."
- "... be able to sustain the collaboration that led to the formation of V8 beyond Year Three of the MDRII program."

Business, commercial/and economic factors, a focus on youth, and improving the physical fabric and quality of life in the target areas were also suggested.

*Perceived strengths*

- There was widespread agreement (83% strongly agreed or agreed) that the collaboratives were working toward a shared vision, with little variation between the three groups.
- Respondents largely strongly agreed (18%) or agreed (59%) that they were engaging a broad and diverse group of stakeholders. However, there was some variation between the three collaborative, from 66% (DGPC) to 80% at Fort/Visger to 89% at V8-Gateway. This is reflective of DGPC's struggle to engage the suburban government to the degree that they would like.
- Overall, 86% of respondents agreed or strongly agreed that they were making significant progress toward aligning goals, plans, and resources, but at the target area results were mixed: 86% of DGPC respondents and 100% of V8-Gateway respondents felt this way, compared to 70% of Fort/Visger respondents.
- Asked about their progress over the previous 6 months, responses were uniformly positive. Respondents in all three target areas felt that they had been done well in developing or maintaining an effective organizational structure, in developing or maintaining an effective relationship with Detroit LISC, and in achieving the goals identified by their stakeholders.

- In general, LISC support was seen positively across all three collaboratives. Respondents were asked to rate LISC support across 11 dimensions from extremely valuable to not valuable at all, as well as "didn't use/attend".
- Respondents were also positive with regard to LISC support in providing responses to questions in a timely manner, providing information or technical support to address race and cultural relations, and facilitating collaboration and relationship-building. Over 60% of respondents rated LISC support very valuable or extremely valuable.

*Mixed perceptions*
- Nearly 50% of respondents said that their views on the relevance or importance of regional and social equity did not change very much, with responses fairly consistent between collaboratives. From our interviews, it appears that this is a reflection of the fact that most participants were aware of the relevance or importance of this issue before they embarked on MDRII.
- When asked about implementing a regional investment strategy, one could perhaps see the challenges that DGPC is facing. Here, 40% of respondents agreed or strongly agreed that they were making significant progress. In comparison, 80% of Fort/Visger respondents and 67% of V8-Gateway respondents felt that they were making significant progress.

*Perceived weaknesses or limitations*
- Sixty-eight percent of respondents indicated that regional equity in their areas was somewhat low or very low, an improvement from the second year when 75% of respondents had indicated a similar sentiment. Looking across the three collaboratives, V8-Gateway respondents had the most positive views, differing significantly from DGPC and Fort/Visger.
- More than two-thirds (67%) of V8 respondents thought that regional equity in their area was moderate or better, compared to 30% in Fort/Visger and 12% in DGPC. Interviews indicate that the very low numbers of DGPC are reflective of the fact that their collaborative contains the greatest contrast between city and suburban neighborhoods.

**Focus group and interview results**

*Perceived strengths*
- The idea of collaboration has broadly evolved into thinking beyond the city–suburb divide: "One of the changes or benefits to the community has occurred not only because of the great community interaction we had predicted as part of our joint application, but there is also a great creative dynamic in place .... Up to this point, prior to the program, what happened in Detroit stayed in Detroit. What happened in Warren—Centerline stayed there. This has been a great movement to be able to amalgamate and overcome the 8 Mile border mentality and to think regionally."
- "I think people are beginning to really think and look at the area more as a region rather than 'I represent this specific city.' They are now looking at how we can come together and how can I pat your back and you pat my back and how together can we move things forward. I feel that it is starting to come together and have a little bit of synergy instead of four separate communities."

- The recognition by LISC of the need for operational support was appreciated. In a participant's words, " ... if we were to stand up alone it would put an extreme amount of stress on us and I don't know if we could cope without some funding of positions like the coordinator and the other components of the MDRII program possible."

*Mixed perceptions*
- The difference between the city and suburban communities was seen as a major factor that distinguished the three collaboratives. One participant said, "I think one issue that sort of unites Gateway and the Fort Visger groups [is] that demographically we're pretty much in the same economic milieu and survival of our neighborhoods, whether it be on the Warren side or the Centerline side or Detroit is pretty much a factor that affects us all. I can't speak for the Grosse Pointe–Detroit side, but we are pretty much in a survival mode."

*Perceived limitations or weaknesses*
- Respondents referred to the political climate in the various units of government involved (or not involved) in the collaboratives. There have been changes in leadership in some of these communities (new mayors, for example), leading to understandable uncertainty on the part of continuing members of the collaborative.
- Another factor, not part of the MDRII process but nonetheless having a profound impact, was the foreclosure crisis. Several community-based organizations have been forced to spend a lot more time than they had anticipated on helping their residents with this issue.
- There is still a sense that the amount of time and work that is required of the process, especially for the lead organizations, far exceeds what they are compensated for through LISC monies. However, the money for administrative support has meant that the situation has improved compared to previous years.

**Discussion: looking across the three sites**

The MDRII began an unprecedented dialogue between Detroit and its inner-ring suburban neighbors. MDRII bridged a gap that had never, in recent history, been bridged before. In two of the three collaboratives, the groups had never met prior to this MDRII process. Three years later, the groups have experienced success – in varying degrees and over longer-than-anticipated time spans. Overall, DGPC and V8-Gateway have developed a shared vision, created trust and real collaboration among partners, and created solid structures. The focus of these groups, while unique to their specific geographic area, remains consistent: a commitment to their target area to coordinate the needed programs, partners, and resources for residents on both sides of the border.

The third group, Fort/Visger, has been the most challenging. While this group brought the most municipalities together, most of the community partners had minimal capacity and only had volunteer staff. Moreover, the history of this area brings with it racial and cultural tension between southwest Detroit and its adjacent communities. The lack of organizational capacity coupled with the tension between the communities and staff turnover with the municipalities made it very difficult to develop trust or collaboration among the members. For the first 12–18 months, Detroit LISC deployed capacity resources to Fort/Visger including staff and consultant time in an effort to develop a structure where a work plan could be developed. While FVC has made some progress, it continues to be a challenge to work in this area.

### *Government-driven versus community-based development*
Participation by local governments was shaped by the interest of the local political leadership, changes in leadership, and severe budget constraints which led to a lot of staff turnover, sometimes limiting attention to this project. Many individual suburban government representatives, by virtue of their personal interest, continued their efforts even when it was very difficult to do so. The City of Detroit was largely absent. The various pressures on governments in these times of fiscal crisis in Michigan, and the inertia of government bureaucracies, are the reasons why collaboration between city and suburban governments is difficult to achieve.

MDRII's community development model, based on small neighborhood-based projects that actively cross jurisdictional boundaries, presents a viable alternative to large-scale regional cooperation by local governments.

### *Collaboration issues must be addressed on a case-by-case basis*
In all three sites, there was unevenness in the capacity of partnering organizations. In general, CDCs on the Detroit side were well-established and had a successful track record. Suburban communities had few, if any, CDCs and were often represented at the table by their local governments. In only one of the three sites, DGPC had there been a history of cross-border collaboration for a commercial project, so in other situations, relationships had to be built from scratch.

Participants spent a large amount of time and effort to create the conditions for effective collaboration, through ensuring diverse representation, leadership reflective of the communities, and participatory and transparent internal processes.

### *The need to confront race head-on*
There is always the specter of race and inequity that is so present in the area. While cross-jurisdictional, collaborative projects create the space for discussing racial inequity, participants were convinced that these projects by themselves do not adequately address racial inequities, and that there is need to confront the issue of race separately from any projects. At the same time, participants felt the discussions on race had greater purpose and substance because of the projects on a parallel track. Participants were very positive about the continuing support provided in this area for each collaborative by the MRDI and New Detroit.

### *The need for strong, consistent support*
All three collaboratives were committed to, but anxious about, the manner in which the work of MDRII will proceed. In interviews, they referred to changes in LISC's

approach and the uncertainty surrounding resources committed to this project. While many are convinced that they will find ways to move the project forward, the participating organizations have no "extra" resources to divert to this work.

**Implications for the field of community development**

*Targeted regional planning can be an effective approach in many communities*

Although the three collaboratives have varying results, it is clear that targeted planning and community development interventions embedded in a broader regional perspective can be effective. In response to a general question about what they expected they hoped to achieve as a result of this project, the largest number of responses referred to their region, and to social and economic equity within that region.

Given the history of racial, social, and economic segregation in Detroit, the lack of regional planning, and the example of the DGPC site where the contrast between city and suburb is stark, participants have the sense that if this collective future can be imagined and acted upon here in Detroit, can it happen most anywhere?

*Critical to establish feasible outcomes*

There are lessons in this project about establishing measurable outcomes and then measuring these outcomes in order to get continued support from funders. Among the outcomes established for MDRII were: visibly improved physical infrastructure that supports regional equity; increased regional and social equity in the area; and improved racial and cultural relations among collaborative partners. All this was to be achieved in 3 years.

It is clear now that these outcomes were wildly ambitious. Much has been accomplished, yet the needle on the outcomes has barely moved. The successes are small but unprecedented. For the first time ever, children from both Detroit and Grosse Pointe Park are participating jointly in a theater program, allowing friendships to develop across deep social divides. For the first time, Detroit and the suburbs of Warren and Center Line have a joint facade improvement program which required them to agree on certain guidelines. A series of summer music concerts brought Detroiters and their suburban neighbors together to hear Motown, swing, and salsa music. While each of these barely scratches the surface of the expected outcomes, they are a reflection of the very hard, invisible work that has gone into MDRII.

**Conclusion**

Funders would be wise to back the work of MDRII by showing a continued commitment to regionalism and regional equity. Even where there are few visible signs, much difficult work has been done in the past 2.5 years, and unless there is a concerted effort to build on this foundation, the gains can be easily lost. All the stakeholders in the process need to take time to put in place a plan for the future of MDRII and regional equity in metro Detroit.

For the region and for the field, MDRII provides an approach to regional planning through community development that is not yet widely used. The conventional view of regional planning is large-scale. This project offers a counter-view that regional planning can be achieved through incremental, small-scale, cross-jurisdictional approaches.

**References**

Center for Justice, Community and Tolerance. (2006). *Edging towards equity: Creating shared opportunity in America's regions: Report on the conversation on regional equity*. Santa Cruz, CA: UC Santa Cruz.

French, R. (2002, January 13). New segregation: Races accept divide. *The Detroit News*. Retrieved from http://www.detnews.com/legacy/specialreports/2002/segregation/a01-389727.htm. Accessed November 30, 2011.

Glover-Blackwell, A., & Fox, R. (2004). *Regional equity and smart growth: Opportunities for advancing social and economic justice in America*. Retrieved from http://www.fundersnetwork.org/usr_doc/Regional_Equity_and_Smart_Growth_2nd_Ed.pdf

Lewis Mumford Center, University of Albany, SUNY. (n.d.). Retrieved from http://www.detroit1701.org/Class_Highest%20Seg%20Table.html

Orfield, M. (2002). *American metropolitics: The new suburban reality*. Washington, DC: The Brookings Institution.

Orfield, M., & Luce, T. (2003). *Michigan metropatterns: A regional agenda for community and prosperity in Michigan*. Minneapolis, MN: Amerigis.

PolicyLink. (2003). *Promise and challenge: Achieving regional equity in greater Boston*. Oakland, CA: PolicyLink.

Puentes, R., & Warren, D. (2006). *One-fifth of America: A comprehensive guide to America's first suburbs*. Washington, DC: The Brookings Institution.

Rusk, D. (1993). *Cities without suburbs*. Baltimore, MD: Johns Hopkins University Press.

Simmons, Z. (2002, January 14). Major moments in metro Detroit race relations. *The Detroit News*. Retrieved from http://www.s4.brown.edu/cen2000/othersay/detroitnews/Stories/Major%20moments%20in%20Metro%20Detroit%20race%20relations%20-%201-14-02.pdf. Accessed November 30, 2011.

# A model to embed health outcomes into land-use planning

Pam Moore

*Interior Health Authority, Health Protection, Canada*

Research links public health outcomes to the built environment. What is not clear is how and to what degree public health agencies can partner with local governments to influence development patterns and urban design. Public health programs tend to emphasis mandated responsibilities such as air quality or waste management. Yet the most beneficial long-term outcomes of improving our built environments – reductions in the prevalence of chronic diseases and injuries, improved senior's health, healthier childhood environments – are affected more by non-mandated aspects of a public health agency's role. British Columbia developed model core programs in public health and the recommendations in the program development resulted in a health authority creating a model for reinventing their role in land-use planning. The Health Authority developed standard approaches for land development using a public health lens based on seven dimensions. The model included developing partnerships with stakeholders – local and provincial governments, agencies and the public – to support the creation of healthier built environments. This paper discusses the initial steps to date and future plans. It includes a summation of two years of practical application of the processes and procedures developed to incorporate health as an explicit expectation of planning and development.

## Background

Research indicates that living and working conditions have the greatest influence on health. Therefore, health is as much a result of our physical health and social environment (which includes having clean drinking water, public safety, transportation, green spaces, schools, healthy work/business environments and housing) as it is a product of the health-care system and health services. (Healthy Municipalities and Communities, n.d.)

Health organizations across Canada are currently faced with escalating acute care costs associated with the increasing prevalence of chronic disease. The trend to put more money into the acute care system is no longer sustainable and alternate solutions to reduce chronic disease prevalence need development. One potential approach is to build upon the relationship between public health and civic planning.

Public health and urban planning have many areas in common, including a population-level focus and the need to deal with complex competing factors.

Identifying and acting on areas in common becomes difficult without a developed process that identifies resources and the capacity to act on opportunities to collaborate with planners and local government.

Historically, local government planning was related to public health through disease prevention, sanitation, and slum eradication. As city centers became densely populated and disease outbreaks increased, people moved out to the suburbs and the beginnings of urban sprawl began. Public health's role with local government shifted from disease prevention and improved sanitation to sustaining infrastructure for issues such as sewage and drinking water. In the process, consideration of the broader health impacts of the built urban form lost focus.

In recent years, there has been increased recognition that a concerted effort is required to reconnect public health and urban planning – driven in part by growing evidence that the built environment is contributing to more unhealthy choices, increased obesity and reduced levels of physical fitness. Incorporating a health perspective into land-use decisions requires creating space for the perspective that there exists an impact of land use on population health. Such a perspective must compete with an already complex process involving multiple stakeholders and divergent or overlapping interests. It also requires that urban planners develop an understanding of the health outcomes associated with the built environment, including its influence on the determinants of health.

An understanding of the Federal and Provincial healthcare system is necessary to identify barriers and opportunities at a regional level for public health staff and urban planners to develop a working relationship.

**The Canadian healthcare system**

The Canadian public healthcare system has a very direct role in the organization of healthcare and resource allocation of healthcare services. Canada's healthcare system is a publicly financed system of public healthcare insurance.

The healthcare system includes the health policies – both for healthcare and other health-related public policies that have a broad scope and encompass healthcare as well as maintaining population health. Canada's current system focuses on the effects of healthcare access and delivery and not on the determinants of health or those factors outside the healthcare sector that influence health status and population health.

The federal, provincial and territorial governments share the responsibility for healthcare. The federal government pays some of the costs of the provincial healthcare programs and outlines some of the rules for provision of health services for the provinces and territories. The provincial and territorial governments are responsible for the administration and delivery of healthcare.

In recent years, another model for healthcare has emerged. This involves the municipal government as a third level of government responsible for healthcare. All provinces have de-centralized their healthcare services to regional bodies. The creation of this model is rooted in the belief that regional healthcare will be more responsive to local health needs and will operate more effectively. The regional structures have the authorization to perform functions previously the responsibility of provincial or local governments.

In the province of British Columbia, public health programming is incorporated as a program within a larger Health Authority (HA) that provides a wide range of health services to residents within a geographic area. The province is divided into five geographic regions each of which have a health authority. Certain provincial activities are provided through a Provincial Health Services Authority (PHSA). Policy oversight and legislative responsibilities are overseen by branches of the provincial government (Ministries), of which two relate directly to public health programming.

The HA was established in 2001 and its role was to ensure that publicly funded health services are provided for the residents. The services include clinical care and community care, which includes public health programs. These programs focus on health promotion, prevention of illness and injury, and protection of the environment, to improve the health of the community rather than just the treatment of illness and disability. This HA serves a large geographic area of approximately 215,000 square kilometers with a mixture of remote areas, rural and smaller urban communities with a total population of 735,000.

In 2005/06 the provincial Ministry of Health initiated the development of Model Core Programs in Public Health. Spurred by the need to address the recommendations included in the Model Core Programs, over the past 18 months the HA has undertaken development of a model for reinventing its role in land-use planning. The HA has developed a model for reviewing civic planning documents applying a population health lens. The approach attempts to educate local government and the public about the health outcomes influenced by the built environment, including the relationship between the built environment and the determinants of health. It identifies the key relationships that need to be developed as well as flagging current and future areas for collaboration and partnership.

In 2007 the HA created a Healthy Community Environment (HCE) position to develop a model for linking health outcomes to land use. The following discussion will describe the development of that model.

## Discussion

### Development of the Health Authority model

The initial phase of the HA's HCE initiative was limited to review of development proposals over 100 housing units submitted by local governments. Planning staff responsible for the individual referrals were contacted by the HCE initiative and a preliminary review template or model used by the HCE initiative evolved from those discussions.

During this period, the PHSA was also developing training workshops for health professionals based on two documents it had developed specifically to address the need for education on health and the built environment: *Foundations for a Healthier Built Environment* (PHSA, 2008a) and *Introduction to Land Use Planning for Health Professionals* (PHSA, 2008b).

These documents were developed to provide health professionals with the basic language of community planning and assist them to recognize the opportunities that existed to become active participants in community planning processes. Such opportunities include involvement in the development of Official Community Plans (OCP) or Regional Growth Strategies (RGS) and master plans related to transportation, parks and recreation. While this was helpful for health professionals in understanding healthier built environments, a need was identified for tools that were usable by public health staff in contributing directly to land-use planning decisions. Previous to the development of this HA model there was limited research on tools and processes used by the public health sector to create healthy community planning.

The HA staff developed standard approaches and templates for land development reviews using a public health lens based on seven dimensions of health. The dimensions are based upon those areas in which health authorities have the expertise and staff to make an informed contribution to discussions on land-use planning. The seven dimensions are as follows:

(1) Environment (air, water).
(2) Injury prevention.
(3) Nutrition and food security.
(4) Healthy child development.
(5) Physical activity as affected by transportation and recreation choices.
(6) Housing and social wellness.
(7) Access and inclusion for those with mental illness or disabilities.

Organizing around these dimensions has reframed land-use planning issues using a public health perspective. It allows the HA to communicate the potential health impacts of land-use planning decisions and to promote and advocate for healthier built environments.

> Public health professionals can provide an institutional voice whose primary focus is human health, a role not played by any of the other institutional players involved in land use decision-making. Public Health officials can consistently ask whether this (land use) will encourage or discourage healthy behaviours. This does not mean that 'health' will become the sole, or necessarily even the primary consideration in all decisions. But it can become a factor that is systematically considered. (Capitol Health Region, 2007)

Public Health's mandate encompasses a broad range of activities focusing on improving the health of the population. As such, it is well positioned to represent the health sector at the land-use decision-making table. Planning support can include identification of regulatory expectations such as sewerage system setbacks, provision of parkland, or better practice approaches to healthier land-use planning. The gradient of regulatory requirement through to better management approaches can be managed in the single review process.

Central to developing a model to entrench health outcomes systematically into processes within a HA and local government was the identification of key stakeholders and the barriers and opportunities for involvement. During the identification process two competing factors emerged – the Climate Action Charter and the Public Health Act – both of which have begun to refocus the model and will be discussed in greater detail.

### *Identification of key stakeholders*
#### Health Authority staff
In 2001 the province of British Columbia amalgamated into the six health authorities. Previously, public health structures were more closely aligned with local

governments and covered smaller geographic areas. The amalgamation resulted in consolidation of services. An unanticipated result of the loss of these local positions was the disruption of, in some cases, very long-term relationships between HA staff and local governments. Interaction between these groups became disjointed and government staff and the public were uncertain of "who to contact" within the HA.

Relationships are being re-established and redefined. Staff currently involved in local government relationships are unfamiliar with historical linkages, and more legislative responsibilities are resulting in staff with a regulator rather than collaborator relationship. The growing body of literature on fostering healthier built environments stresses the key necessity of building strong personal relationships between employees of the health authority and other stakeholders, particularly municipal planning staff and local elected officials. In order to nurture that relationship-building, the HA recognized that it would need to identify the key internal staff involved in planning and delivering public health programs and to clearly articulate their roles in regard to promoting healthier built environments.

An advantage of the integrated HA was a common umbrella that allowed bringing together key staff involved in environmental health, population health, family health, child and youth health, mental health and addictions, and persons with disabilities (including seniors). Each of these professionals utilizes a variety of public engagement and collaborative styles. An Environmental Health Officer's regulatory role has an outcome evidence-based response. Population health takes an upstream approach and develops partnerships at the community level to foster change. Public Health Nurses and Home/Community Care staff work with individuals, groups, or at the community level. Mental Health and Addictions workers identify key issues, raise awareness of those issues and then identify coalitions to increase system capacity to move those issues forward. Medical Health Officers provide a system wide understanding, community leadership, and leadership amongst healthcare providers.

Once the key professionals were identified and support obtained from their program areas, the HA was able to develop a strategy for linking the disparate foci of each into a coherent model to support efforts to create healthier built environments. The key components of developing this system-wide approach are as follows.

*Demonstrating the HCE initiative's policies and templates relevance to all other programs.* (Montreal Network of Health Promoting Hospitals and CSSSs, 2009). Each key health professional has varying levels of knowledge of local government and community planning structure, language and process. Initial groundwork included contacting individual staff within key programs to discuss the built environment and its links to population health outcomes. This helped broaden staff's understanding both of their program's mandates and how those mandates were connected to the built environment and community planning.

The HCE initiative engaged management within each key program on issues of the fundamental concepts of land-use planning, and the links between the determinants of health and a healthy built environment. The engagement also included a program description of the HCE initiative. Management of each program area was asked what its members perceived could be their involvement in supporting healthy built environments.

The goal of this component was to ensure that staff in the key program areas were familiar with:

- the concepts of a healthy built environment as it impacts population health;
- the determinants of health;
- the existing programs within the HA that were working in this subject area;
- the appropriate contacts within the HA for the public or local government to contact with questions/comments and/or requests for support regarding planning and health outcomes;
- the HCE initiative information available on the HA public website (PH website, 2009);
- how the guidelines being developed for each of the seven health dimensions (see Discussion section) might affect them in their jobs; and
- how they themselves could use their areas of expertise to actively participate in the review and development of the guidelines for the seven health dimensions.

*Ensuring that the consultation process with the stakeholders is viewed as credible and legitimate.* (Montreal Network of Health Promoting Hospitals and CSSSs, 2009). It was critical to secure the "buy in" of senior management within each of the key programs in order to gain their support for the involvement of their staff. Medical Health Officers were engaged in the process and helped to filter the message from the top down about the "new direction" the HA was taking in promoting a healthy built environment.

*Optimizing communication and consultation activities.* (Montreal Network of Health Promoting Hospitals and CSSSs, 2009). The HCE initiative was involved in three workshops with planning staff and health professionals. The format for each of these workshops included the following:

- introductory remarks by a Medical Health Officer emphasizing the importance of the built environment and its impacts on health;
- presentation of empirical evidence of the role of health and the built environment;
- a summary of planning tools and processes from the *Introduction to Land Use Planning for Health Professionals* (PHSA, 2008b) workshop reader;
- presentation on how the HCE initiative has been involved with local government, including an overview of the development of the template the HA now uses for land-use reviews;
- a sample review of a development proposal using the HA land review template; and
- breakout sessions in which groups rotate through various case studies, allowing them to put into practice the theories that had been presented.

*Development of guidance papers, public webpages, information sheets and geographic information system tools.* An important element in this program was the development of information that could be made available to the public, local government and HA staff. Background information for many of the seven dimensions included in the HA land-use review template, PowerPoint presentations and PHSA documents are now available on the HA website (PH website, 2009).

The benefits of making information widely available include that this:

- provides consistency of health messaging;
- supports HA and local government staff to inform themselves and others quickly about healthy built environment issues; and
- maintains up-to-date information in one location.

The guideline papers for the seven dimensions provide HA staff with the context within which they can understand and be actively involved in formalizing their own roles within the HCE initiative. In doing so, they help to clarify their own program's guiding principles and core values as they relate to promoting a healthy built environment.

An example of an internal process that has developed from the HCE initiative model is active transportation initiatives. Many local governments are reviewing active transportation (cycling/walking trails, community walkability, and school walkability) as part of reducing their greenhouse gas (GHG) emissions and reducing community member's vehicle dependency. The HCE initiative has had the most community involvement with active transportation initiatives and now has an information sheet that is available to the public/local government linking active transportation to health (HA, 2009). The process includes:

- a request by a local government to become involved in a specific active transportation initiative;
- the HA decides who will respond and with what level of involvement (attending every meeting and community event, via email, etc.); and
- completion of the HA involvement results in a detailed localized report based on what issues were identified during the consultation and linking those issues to health outcomes.

A geographic information system-based evaluation tool as part of the toolkit for land-use reviews is under development. This tool will allow staff to review information for a regional district, municipality, or neighborhood in relation to long-range planning or current planning proposals. The information could include the location of amenities, industry, socio-economic mapping, or early development instrument evaluations. This tool would give staff a more complete overview of a location when reviewing proposals.

Currently within a one-kilometer radius the following information about individual development proposals is available:

- population density;
- percentage of homes rented versus owned;
- percentage of children aged zero to four, and aged zero to nine; and
- type of road class (i.e. local road, arterial).

Discussions are underway with some of the local governments, the Public Health Agency of Canada, and the Human Early Learning Partnership (n.d.) with the early development instrument to discuss sharing of data for the following information within a one-kilometer radius:

- recreation facilities and food stores;
- land use, including green space and walking/biking trails;
- current transit routes; and
- early development instrument data at the neighborhood level.

The Regional HAs are mandated to provide local governments with health profiles for their geographical area. Within this HA, the local health area profiles provides an overview of residents in the HA and highlights key characteristics in the following areas:

- Health status – mortality, life expectancy, leading cause of death, chronic disease, and health behavior.
- Health system performance – age-standardized day rates, inpatient referral patterns.
- Health services – type of services available in the HA.

The health indicators conceptual framework developed by the Canadian Institute for Health Information reflects the principle that health is determined not only by medical care, but by individual and population level, social and economic factors.

The information provided in the local health area profiles is currently of limited use to a local government to be able to affect change within their planning processes. The information, for example, does not allow a planner to identify areas or population groups where obesity rates have increased from previous reporting periods and use that information to create more green space or parks within their community or at the development level to influence recreation programming. The Information Support Services within this HA have recognized that provision of useful information linked to the built environment is invaluable to a local government. Currently discussions are underway to determine the type of health information from various data sources that can be made available to local governments and the depth of geographical scale that health information can be collected.

*Local government staff*

*Planners, council and consultants.* Literature abounds on the need for health professional and planners to collaborate and work together towards a common goal of fostering healthy built environments (PHSA, 2008b). Planners have readily identified the effects of the built environment on health, but the literature is currently lacking regarding HA initiatives resulting in improved health outcomes in the built environment, compounding challenges to facilitate change.

To date it has been difficult to determine the effect the HA's review process has had on planners understanding the broad concepts of health and how this overlaps with land-use planning. For example, planning language typically does not encompass social, mental or physical health, while public health language does not include bricks and mortar. To date, efforts by the HCE initiative to have public health language incorporated into community planning documents have not been effective. Part of the reason for this may lie in the local government process itself. Some of the reasons for this might be as follows:

(1) Planners focus on the physical pattern of communities, land-use planning policies relate to form, character and design of communities and related

infrastructure. Inherent in these policies is the opportunity for communities to be active and maintain healthy weights but it is not explicitly stated.

(2) The relationship developed with planners and the HCE initiative is at the mid-management level. Although there have been discussions with Directors of Planning and higher level staff, the day-to-day working relationship is with mid-level planning staff. Their ability to affect change is minimal as decisions for process change are made at higher management levels in local governments. Attempts to discuss and develop a more in-depth working process with Health and Planning Departments are ongoing.

(3) The Local Government Act (LGA, 2010) governs the processes for local government and details the agencies that must be consulted for their input into an OCP or RGS. A regional HA is not explicitly identified as one of the agencies to be consulted and as a result a HA is not consistently consulted for input into long-range planning processes.

(4) The LGA-established content for an OCP includes social needs, social well-being and social development. A RGS is not as descriptive and requires a comprehensive statement that includes social objectives. "Social" is not defined within the LGA as including health outcomes and it results in local government inconsistently defining social outcomes for their communities (LGA).

(5) Many local governments hire consultants to draft specific land use policies. Typically, a local government drafts a terms of reference document outlining:

- projects goals – what will the project accomplish;
- objectives – may include specific matters to be addressed and scope of the project;
- expected results – description of the information to be included in the report; and
- proposal requirements – expectations by local government for the consultant (e.g. project schedule).

If the TOR does not explicitly include health outcomes in the goals, objectives, or results, there is no impetus for the consultant to broaden their knowledge of the interplay between health and the built environment, or to include health outcomes in their draft policies, or include HA staff in a stakeholders group.

Typically, a consultant will form a stakeholders group of interested parties, including community groups, neighborhood associations and potentially health staff. Ideally, these stakeholders groups should ensure that all commonly held opinions within the group are brought forward and become part of the policies being developed. Unfortunately, in reality the process is seldom so inclusive. Usually, broad vision statements are created and eventually refined to more specific goal statements. To date, there had been no specific inclusion of health outcomes in any of the stakeholders' draft documents.

(6) HA staff readily distinguish regulatory from collaborative health improvement initiatives; however, local governments confuse the roles and may only perceive HA involvement in association with regulatory requirements that can be barriers to progressive built environment decisions.

*Identification of competing factors.* During the period of identification of stakeholders and barriers/opportunities for involvement, two competing factors or drivers for change were identified. The Climate Action Charter and the Public Health Act are new provincial legislation and their impact on creating healthy community planning is yet to be defined.

*Climate Action Charter.* The Climate Action Charter (BC Climate Action Charter, 2007) and Local Government (Green Communities) Legislative Amendments (Bill 27, 2008) are two of the legislative documents designed to encourage local governments to reduce GHG. The legislation establishes local governments' land-use policies and processes that promote a compact built environment with less vehicle dependency and overall energy use. In 2007 the provincial government and local government shared their commitment to reducing GHGs by voluntarily agreeing to:

- set targets to reduce their GHGs by developing policies and actions to achieve those targets in their Official Community Plan by 31 May 2010 or Regional Growth Strategy by 31 May 2011;
- commit to becoming carbon neutral with their operation by 2012; and
- reduce their GHGs by 33% below the 2007 levels by 2020, and 80% by 2050.

To assist local government, a Community Energy and Emissions Inventory (BC Community Energy and Emissions Inventory Initiative, 2007) was completed for each municipality or regional district to provide a 2007 baseline emission inventory. It is estimated that local governments have control or influence over approximately 45% or more of these emissions. The 2007 Community Energy and Emissions Inventory Reports represent high-level estimated community energy consumption and GHG emissions from on-road transportation, buildings, solid waste and land-use change. Two of those areas targeted for GHG reductions – transportation and land use – directly affect health and are linked to the built environment.

The strategies to reduce community GHGs are an area that a HA can become actively involved. The largest community GHG emission source is the personal vehicle. To encourage residents to change their transportation choice to an alternate mode will require the efforts of many key stakeholders collectively working together to create messaging and actions to make alternate transportation modes an easier choice. Local governments working alone and creating active transportation options is only one part of a strategy for change.

An example of this is the planning department for the largest urban centre within the HA has recently stated that, based on a predicted population growth:

> Reducing community greenhouse gases (GHG) is very challenging – especially when the reductions being targeted are as significant as what's been set out by the Province. In essence, within 10 years, every resident will need to have reduced their GHG footprint by 50%. The associated infrastructure and service delivery implications are significant. It is suggested that the multiple bottom line implications be fully explored and reviewed with stakeholders, through the OCP review and the associated 20 year Servicing Plan and Financing Strategy review to be undertaken in the upcoming months. (Kelowna City Council, 2009, p. 2)

The societal shift away from vehicle dependency that will be required for this municipality to achieve its community GHG target is one of the factors that have been identified on which the HCE initiative could capitalize. From a health perspective reducing vehicle dependency results in increasing physical activity opportunities and improving individual health outcomes. The results and benefits of reducing personal vehicle use are different from a local government (GHG reduction) and HA (prevalence of chronic disease) perspective but it does highlight how creating partnerships and working together can achieve improved health outcomes.

Local governments will probably struggle in the next 10 years to reduce their GHGs in their own operations and within the community. They will need to make hard decisions that may not be well received by their citizens. Ultimately, the effectiveness of strategies to adapt to climate change will depend on public and professional buy-in. This will require collaboration with HAs, municipalities and other agencies responsible for individual and public health. To achieve success in creating effective policies for adaptation strategies, there will need to be an even greater emphasis placed on developing inclusive planning processes. This HCE model is supporting local governments to identify and describe the multidisciplinary approaches and involvement needed to move a community towards healthier environments:

> Engagement is key to moving individuals and community leaders forward in developing adaptive strategies to deal with climate change as it unfolds, because it is only when individuals in communities feel vulnerable to the impacts of climate change and understand that their community livelihood and their health may be threatened, that they will be moved to make individual changes and press their communities for adaptive strategies. (Pacific Institute for Climate Solutions, 2008)

HAs are well placed as an impartial accredited source of information to help support and collaborate with a local government to begin the process of a societal shift toward healthier behaviors. The results of this collaboration will benefit both local government and the HA by reducing GHGs and improving health outcomes. The history of tobacco control is an example of successful cross-sectoral collaboration. As different sectors (health, media, local governments, tax policies, and school programs) sequentially gave the warning signs of tobacco use and its health implications, the smoking rates have dropped significantly in areas where comprehensive policies have been implemented.

*Public Health Act.* In 2008 a new Public Health Act was enacted that replaced outdated legislation and began the modernization of public health. The Act expanded and redefined public health issues such as communicable disease prevention and control, health promotion and health protection, chronic disease and injury prevention. The Act redefines the term "health hazard" and introduces the term "health impediment" (Appendix 1). The significance of these definitions to identifying health outcomes within the planning and development process is yet to be determined by the HAs.

The Act also sets out a new direction for local governments by defining their role to ensure the health of the community with requirements that include:

- designation of a local government person as a health liaison to a regional health authority; and
- requirement of local government action if it becomes aware of a health hazard or health impediment (Appendix 2, (1) (2) (4)).

Processes for HA involvement have not yet been developed and are dependent upon direction from the provincial government.

The Public Health Act expands the role of the Medical Health Officer to include advising and reporting on public health issues of a much wider scope. (Appendix 3) The impact of these duties by a Medical Health Office has not been determined.

The implication of the new direction for the Public Health Act will impact on a HA and local government's relationship. This HA has determined that as a precursor to establishing a working relationship, the HA will determine what tools they can offer to a local government in the form of data collection and information exchange. It is invaluable for a local government to understand the health of their population with indicators that relate to chronic diseases linked with the built environment. Health information tied to easily understood definitions and their significance to land use is a valuable tool for a local government when developing long-range plans or at the individual development stage.

**Conclusion**

The HCE initiative has created land-use review templates, established internal processes for informing and mobilizing HA staff and laid out a framework for developing positive working relationships with local government's staff and elected officials. Planners have been informed of the HCE initiative's goals and health information has been made available to them. Progress has been made, and several local governments in the region have proactively included public health at stakeholders' tables. The HCE initiative is currently involved with review of development proposals, OCP and RGS.

In theory, many of the recommendations made on how to undertake support for healthy built environments have been or are in the process of being implemented. However, in practice it is not evident that real change has occurred and that health outcomes have become a standard consideration when making land-use decisions.

The question then becomes:

- What else needs to be done to build the partnership between public health and local government that will ultimately result in healthy built environments?
- What could be added to the existing process to move both local governments and the HA in this direction?

*What are the next steps for the Health Authority?*

One of the goals of the HA is to:

> Improve the health of the population, prevent communicable and chronic disease, reduce injury and disability, and protect the public from harm caused by environmental factors. (HA, 2009/2010)

The HA is well positioned to offer its support to local governments and their goals of creating healthy and vibrant communities. As described in this paper, there are currently many health professionals that have some role to play in fostering healthy built environments.

The next steps for the HA are as follows:

- Build on the existing capacity internally to increase the knowledge base of staff on their role in fostering healthy built environments;

- continue to develop guidance papers and information sheets on key health outcome concepts as they relate to the built environment;
- create engagement opportunities with local government to discuss options for adaptation strategies to reduce GHGs;
- work with local government to determine the type and scope of data that will help support a local government to embed health outcomes into land-use decisions;
- develop an internal strategy for working with local government health liaisons;
- clarify at a provincial level the connection of health hazard and health impediment to the built environment;
- link with interested outside partners including community groups, researchers and other government agencies to develop working relationships;
- develop meaningful working relationships with planners and other government staff to link health outcomes to land-use planning; and
- work with elected officials to understand the linkages of health outcomes to the built environment.

The HCE initiative has developed standard approaches and templates for land development reviews using a public health lens and established internal processes for informing and mobilizing HA staff. Planners have been informed of the HCE initiative's goals and health information has been made available to them. A framework has been established for developing positive working relationships with local government staff and elected officials.

Legislative changes provincially and within local governments have been identified that may impact the future working relationships of health authority staff and local governments.

The HCE initiative has recognized that both within a HA and within local governments, current processes and procedures impact the ability of embedding health outcomes into land-use decisions. The processes and procedures have been identified and can be used in the future as a reference point for further discussions with local governments.

**References**

BC Climate Action Charter. (2007). Retrieved from http://www.cd.gov.bc.ca/ministry/docs/climate_action_charter.pdf

BC Community Energy and Emissions Inventory Initiative. (2007). Retrieved from http://www.env.gov.bc.ca/epd/climate/ceei/reports.htm

Bill 27. (2008). *Local Government (Green Communities) Statutes Amendment Act.* Retrieved from http://www.leg.bc.ca/38th4th/1st_read/gov27-1.htm

Capitol Health Region. (2007, September). *Designing healthy places – Land use planning and public health.* Retrieved from http://www.capitalhealth.ca/nr/rdonlyres/eh4qelt76mejjm xogexsmbh5qrs32flyyiknqr3z6jn6xcfgyjqbeqpip3xrsztvr27joqqj2bd2pyr7myh74cnflib/ designinghealthyplaceslandusepublication.pdf

Human Early Learning Partnership, Early Development Instrument. (n.d.). Retrieved from http://www.earlylearning.ubc.ca/EDI

Health Authority. (2009). *Active transportation and health.* Retrieved fromfhttp://www.interiorhealth.ca/uploadedFiles/Choose_Health/Healthy_Aging/Newsletters/ActiveTrans.pdf

Healthy Authority. (2009/10). *Goals and strategies.* Retrieved from http://inet.interiorhealth.ca/clinical/PH/admin/Documents/PH%20strategy%202009-10%20to%202011-12.pdf

Healthy Municipalities and Communities. (n.d.). *Mayors guide for promoting quality of life. Pan American Health Organization.* Retrieved from http://www.paho.org/English/AD/SDE/HS/MCS_Guide.pdf

Kelowna City Council. (2009, November). *Presentation to City Council.* Retrieved from http://www.kelowna.ca/CityPage/Docs/PDFs/%5CCouncil%5CMeetings%5CCouncil%20Meetings%202009%5C2009%2D11%2D30/Item%208%2E1%20%2D%20Kelowna%20Community%20Greenhouse%20Gas%20Emissions%20Inventory%20and%20Projections%2Epdf

Local Government Act. (2010, June). Retrieved from http://www.bclaws.ca/EPLibraries/bclaws_new/document/ID/freeside/96323_00

Montreal Network of Health Promoting Hospitals and CSSSs. (2009). *Guide to develop a health promotion policy and compendium of policies.* Retrieved fom http://www.cmis.mtl.rtss.qc.ca/pdf/publications/isbn978-2-89510-320-2.pdf

Pacific Institute for Climate Solutions. (2008, November). *Climate change and health in British Columbia.* Retrieved from http://www.pics.uvic.ca/assets/pdf/publications/Health.pdf

Provincial Health Service Authority. (2008a). *Foundations for a healthier built environment.* Retrieved from http://www.phsa.ca/HealthProfessionals/Population-Public-Health/Healthy-Built-Environment/default.htm

Provincial Health Services Authority. (2008b). *Introduction to land use planning for health professionals.* Retrieved from http://www.phsa.ca/NR/rdonlyres/B874A0D9-398F-4B44-A0D5-32634328EBAB/0/IntroductiontoLandUsePlanningforHealthProfessionalsWorkshopReader.pdf

Public Health website. (2009). *Health & safety – healthy community environments.* Retrieved from http://www.interiorhealth.ca/health-and-safety.aspx?id=7874

## Appendix 1. Definitions

"health hazard" means

- (a) a condition or thing or an activity that
    - (i) endanger, or is likely to endanger public health
    - (ii) interferes, or is likely to interfere, with the suppression of infectious agents or hazardous agents, or

- (b) prescribed condition, thing or activity, including a prescribed condition, thing or activity that
    - (i) is associated with injury or illness, or
    - (ii) fails to meet a prescribed standard in relationship to health, injury or illness

"health impediment" means a prescribed condition, thing, or activity

- (a) the cumulative effects of which, over a period of times, are likely to adversely affect public health
- (b) that causes significant chronic disease or disability in the population
- (c) that interferes with or is inconsistent with the goals of public health initiatives respecting the prevention of injury or illness in the population, including chronic disease or disability, or
- (d) that is associated with poor health within the population

## Appendix 2. Section 120: Regulations respecting local governments

120 (1) The Lieutenant Governor in Council may make regulations under this section in respect of local governments for one or more of the following purposes:

(a) to promote or protect the health of the people within the jurisdiction of the local government;

(b) to address a condition, thing or activity that could adversely affect a health promotion or health protection initiative;
(c) to enforce a memorandum of understanding or other arrangement made under this section.
(2) The Lieutenant Governor in Council may make regulations as follows:
(a) requiring or authorizing a local government to take one or more actions for the purposes of
(i) monitoring its jurisdiction for a health hazard or health impediment, and
(ii) responding to a health hazard or health impediment;
(b) requiring a local government to deliver a public health function, and, for this purpose, the Lieutenant Governor in Council may do the things described in section 125 (4);
(c) authorizing the minister to order a local government to modify or rescind a bylaw, or an operational or strategic plan or planning process;
(d) establishing processes to resolve disputes between local governments and health authorities in relation to matters under this Act.
(3) For the purposes of a regulation made under subsection (2) (a) or (b), the minister may enter into a memorandum of understanding or other arrangement with a local government establishing alternatives to the obligations that would otherwise be applicable under the regulation.
(4) If, by a regulation or order under this Act, the Lieutenant Governor in Council
(a) imposes a duty on one or more local governments, or
(b) authorizes the minister to order one or more local governments to modify or rescind a bylaw, or an operational or strategic plan or planning process, the minister must consult with the affected local governments before the regulation or order is made.
(5) If a regulation or order to which subsection (4) applies affects local governments generally, consultation with the Union of British Columbia Municipalities is effective consultation in respect of municipalities and regional districts.
(6) For the purposes of subsection (4), the minister must
(a) provide sufficient information respecting the proposed regulation or order, and
(b) allow sufficient time before the proposed regulation or order is made for the affected local governments or the Union of British Columbia Municipalities, as applicable, to consider the proposed regulation or order and provide comments to the minister.
(7) The minister must consider any comments provided under subsection (6) and, if requested by an affected local government or, if applicable, the Union of British Columbia Municipalities must respond to those comments.
(8) The minister may require an individual to make an oath or affirmation of confidentiality before the individual may participate in consultations under this section.
(9) Nothing in this section prevents a person who has authority to make an order under this Act to make the order in respect of a local government.

## Appendix 3. Section 73: Advising and reporting on local public health issues

73 (1) In this section:
"**authority**" means a health authority, or a school board or francophone school board under the *School Act*, that has full or partial jurisdiction over a designated area;
"**designated area**" means the geographic area for which a medical health officer has been designated;
"**local government**" means a local government that has full or partial jurisdiction over a designated area.
(2) A medical health officer must monitor the health of the population in the designated area and, for this purpose, may conduct an inspection under Division 1 *[Inspections]* of Part 4.

(3) A medical health officer must advise, in an independent manner, authorities and local governments within the designated area
   (a) on public health issues, including health promotion and health protection,
   (b) on bylaws, policies and practices respecting those issues, and
   (c) on any matter arising from the exercise of the medical health officer's powers or performance of his or her duties under this or any other enactment.
(4) If a medical health officer believes it would be in the public interest to make a report to the public on a matter described in subsection (2) or (3), the medical health officer must
   (a) consult with the provincial health officer and each authority and local government who may reasonably be affected by the intended report, and
   (b) after consultation under paragraph (a), make the report to the extent and in the manner that the medical health officer believes will best serve the public interest.
(5) If requested by the provincial health officer, a medical health officer must make a report to the provincial health officer of advice provided under subsection (3).
(6) A health authority must do all of the following:
   (a) designate a medical health officer to report, respecting the geographic area for which the health authority is responsible,
      (i) on the health of the population within the geographic area, and
      (ii) on the extent to which population health targets established by the government, if applicable, or by the health authority, if any, have been achieved;
   (b) require the medical health officer to report to the health authority at least once each year; publish each report made under this subsection.
(7) A medical health officer who makes a report under subsection (6) may include in the report recommendations relevant to health promotion and health protection in the geographic area for which the health authority is responsible.

# Index

**Note:** Bold face page numbers refer to tables or figures. Page numbers along with "n" refer to foot notes.

Advancing Regional Equity 5
advocacy coalitions 63
African American community 19
age-adjusted death rates 43, **44**
Allegheny Conference on Community Development 14
Alter Road Transformation (ART) 84
anti-poverty policy 36
ART *see* Alter Road Transformation
Atlanta Neighborhood Development Partnership 15

Bay Area Alliance for Sustainable Communities 15
Bay Area Family of Funds 15
Black Panther Party 10
Boston Foundation 49
Boston Health Care and Research Training Institute 50
Boston Private Industry Council 50
Boston Redevelopment Authority (BRA) 51
BRA *see* Boston Redevelopment Authority
"bricks and mortar" approach 7
Building Healthy Communities program 56–7
Bus Riders Union 14

California Endowment 57
Campaign for a Sustainable Milwaukee (CSM) 16
Canadian public healthcare system 93–4
capabilities approach 35–6
CDC *see* community development corporation
Center for Community Change 21
Center on Urban and Metropolitan Policy (CUMP) 65
Central Labor Council 16, 22
CHC *see* Community Health Center
Chicago Housing Authority 29
Cities Targeted Neighborhood Program 69

Citizen Participation Plan 71
civil rights movement 18, 81
Clean Water Act 56
Climate Action Charter 95, 100–2
community-based organizations 1, 38
community-based participatory research framework 55
community-based strategies 45, 49; addressing health disparities 49–55; community development issues and health disparities 45–7; metropolitan segregation and health disparities 43–5; salutogens and pathogens in human ecosystems 48–9
community-based *versus* government-driven development 89
community-benefits agreements 10, 21
"community building" initiatives 7
community building movement 81
Community Capital Investment Initiative 15
community development: corporation 54; implications for 90; and planning initiatives 47; programs 48; use of 47
community development corporation (CDC) 7, 8, 84
community development movement 7
community development regionalism 4, 5–6, 6, 7–8
community economic development policies 34
Community Energy and Emissions Inventory 101
community GHG emission 101
community groups 17–18
Community Health Center (CHC) 53
community-owned and managed research (COMR) approach 55
community revitalization 4
Community Scholars Program 17
"Compatible Institutional Growth" initiative 68
comprehensive community-centered strategy 57
comprehensive community initiatives 7
COMR approach *see* community-owned and managed research approach
constituency mobilization 6
consultants 99–100

109

# INDEX

consultation process, with stakeholders 97
"Cool Cities" initiative 78
council 99–100
Council on Affordable Housing 28
CSM *see* Campaign for a Sustainable Milwaukee
"cultural motivation" 36
culture of poverty 33
CUMP *see* Center on Urban and Metropolitan Policy
CUMP index 65–7, 73; Davenport, Iowa 69; Omaha, Nebraska 71; Springfield, Missouri 67–8; Wichita, Kansas 70
Curb Appeal for Business program 84

Davenport, Iowa: CUMP index 69; urban sprawl 69–70; *USA Today*'s sprawl index 69
Detroit community 18
Detroit–Grosse Pointe Collaborative (DGPC) 18, 83–4, 88
Detroit Local Initiatives Support Corporation (LISC) 16, 18, 78–9; Executive Steering Committee 83
Detroit, regional equity framing 80–1; segregation 80; sprawl 79–80
DGPC *see* Detroit–Grosse Pointe Collaborative
Disparities Project 51
dispersal policy 29
dispersal programs 29–30
dispersal strategy 26
DOT *see* US Department of Transportation

ecologic pathogens 48
economic pathogens 48
economic segregation 80
Eight Mile Road 84
"elite persuasion" 9
environmental health policies 47
Environment Justice Executive Order 12898 55
equity regionalism 2, 32; self-identify 26
equity regionalist 32; perspective 33; policy 34; program 26; strategies 35
ethnic segregation 49
Executive Steering Committee, LISC 83

Fair Housing Act 27
fair share housing programs 27–9
family-support programs 7
FCDC *see* Fenway Community Development Corporation
Federal and Provincial healthcare system 93
federal government, healthcare programs 93
Federal Interagency Working Group 53
federal regional Sustainable Communities 2
Fenway Community Development Corporation (FCDC) 50
Ford Foundation 78, 82

Fort/Visger collaborative 85, 88–9
Fruitvale Transit Village 7
Fund for Our Economic Future 15
Future Land Use Plan 72

Gahegan, Patrick 20
Gamaliel Foundation 21
Gamaliel network 12
Gautreaux program 29
geographic information system-based evaluation tool, development of 97–8
ghetto culture 33
GHG emissions *see* greenhouse gas emissions
government-centered approach, urban sprawl 74
government-driven *versus* community-based development 89
greenhouse gas (GHG) emissions, reduction of 101–2
"green wedge" rural zoning designation policy 71
Gross Pointe Park 18
Growth Management and Land Use Plan 68
Growth Management Institute, The 63
growth management, urban sprawl 75
guidance papers, development of 97–8

HA *see* Health Authority
HCE *see* Healthy Community Environment
Health Authority (HA): goals of 103; model, development of 94–5; public health programs 92–4; standard approaches for land development 92; steps for 103–4
Health Authority, integrated 96
health authority staff 95–9
healthcare system, Canadian public 93–4
health dimensions 95
health disparities: community-based strategies to address 49–55; community development issues and 45–7; metropolitan segregation and 43–5
health hazards, definition 105
health impact assessments (HIAs) 57
Health Impact Project 58n3
health impediment 102; definition 105
health indicators conceptual framework 99
health organizations in Canada 92
health policies 93
health services 99
health status 99
health system performance 99
Healthy Community Environment (HCE) 94; initiative 96, 103–4
HIAs *see* health impact assessments
Highway Corridor Overlay District, planned development 69
Historic Preservation Plan 70–1

# INDEX

historic racial inequalities 18
Home/Community Care staffs 96
HOPE VI 29–30, 33
Human Early Learning Partnership 98
human ecosystems 47; features of 48; salutogens and pathogens in 48–9

IMC fertilizer plant *see* International Mineral and Chemicals fertilizer plant
inclusionary zoning (IZ) 28
information sheets, development of 97–8
Information Support Services 99
integrated Health Authority, advantage of 96
International Mineral and Chemicals (IMC) fertilizer plant 52
IZ *see* inclusionary zoning

Jamaica Plain Neighborhood Development Corporation (JPNDC) 49–51, 50, 51
JCS staff *see* Office of Jobs and Community Services staff
Joint Venture: Silicon Valley (JV:SV) 13, 14
JPNDC *see* Jamaica Plain Neighborhood Development Corporation
JV:SV *see* Joint Venture: Silicon Valley

Kerner Commission 26
"Key Transportation Corridors" policy and planned development 68
Korean communities 20

LAANE *see* Los Angeles Alliance for a New Economy
labor and community groups 18
labor/community alliances 16–17
land development, standard approaches for 92, 95
landmark community benefits agreements 20
Land Use Concept Plan 72
land-use planning: dimensions of health 95; health authority role in 92, 94; planners and 99–100
Latino immigrants 20
leadership development and training programs 17
LGA *see* Local Government Act
liberal expansionism 26
LISC *see* Detroit Local Initiatives Support Corporation
Livable Neighborhoods Coalition 18
Livonia 81
LMA Interim Guidelines 51
Local Government Act (LGA) 100
Local Government (Green Communities) Legislative Amendments 101
local government staff: Climate Action Charter 100–2; competing factors identification 100;
planners, council and consultants 99–100; Public Health Act 102–3
local public health issues 106–7
Los Angeles Alliance for a New Economy (LAANE) 14
low-income groups 36

market-based approach, urban sprawl 74
MDRII *see* Metro Detroit Regional Investment Initiative
Medical Health Officers 96; Public Health Act, role of 103
Mental Health and Addictions workers 96
Metro Detroit Regional Investment Initiative (MDRII) 78, 81; collaboration issues 89; DGPC 83–4, 88; focus group and interview results 87–8; Fort/Visger collaborative 85, 88–9; government-driven *versus* community-based development 89; need for strong, consistent support 89–90; planning process 82; process structuring 83; racial inequities 89; site selection 82–3; survey results 86–7; V8-Gateway 84–5, 88
metropolitan jurisdictional fragmentation 45
Metropolitan Policy Program 8
metropolitan segregation, and health disparities 43–5
metropolitan-wide mobility program 29
Michigan Land Use Institute 83
Michigan, regional equity framing 80–1; segregation 80; sprawl 79–80
Michigan Roundtable on Diversity and Inclusion (MRDI) 83
Michigan Suburbs Alliance (MSA) 82, 83
Milwaukee Jobs Initiative 16
Mission Hill Network 50
Mitchell, Harold 52, 54
mobility programs 31; case of 33
mobility strategy 26
Model Core Programs, development of 94
Montgomery County ordinance 28–9
MOSES 16, 20
MOSIAC 84
Moving to Opportunity (MTO) demonstration program 29
MRDI *see* Michigan Roundtable on Diversity and Inclusion
MSA *see* Michigan Suburbs Alliance
MTO demonstration program *see* Moving to Opportunity demonstration program
multi-jurisdictional decision-making 13
municipal government, healthcare programs 93

National Academy of Sciences committee 26
National Center for Health Statistics mortality data 43

# INDEX

natural goods 33
NCDOT *see* North Carolina Department of Transportation
"neighborhood schools" concept 68
"Neighborhoods Element" 68
Neighborhoods Revitalization Plan 70
New Jersey approach 28
new regionalism 25
North Carolina Department of Transportation (NCDOT) 54, 55

OCP *see* Official Community Plans
Office of Jobs and Community Services (JCS) staff 51
Official Community Plans (OCP) 94, 100
Omaha by Design plan 72–3
Omaha, Nebraska: CUMP index 71; urban sprawl 71–3; *USA Today*'s sprawl index 71
Orfield, Myron 9
outcomes, community development 90
Outstanding Neighborhood Enterprise (O.N.E. Youth) 84

Partnership for Working Families 21
pathogens: categories of 48; in human ecosystems, salutogens and 48–9
PHSA *see* Provincial Health Services Authority
place-based strategy 56
place-centric systems approach 48
planners 99–100, 103, 104
planning process, MDRII 82
policy change regionalism 4
policy communities 62
policy entrepreneur approach 9
"policy entrepreneur" form 8
Policy Entrepreneurship 101 9
policy-led regionalism 14
PolicyLink 4
PolicyLink Regional Equity Summits 1
policy reform: regionalism 6, 7, 8–9; strategists 6
political constraints 32
Practical Home and Garden program 84
primary goods 33–4
progressive regionalism 11
provincial government, healthcare programs 93
Provincial Health Services Authority (PHSA) 94
public health: Canadian 93–4; dimensions of 95; local government planning 93; and urban planning 92–3
Public Health Act 95, 102–3
Public Health Agency of Canada 98
public health issues 106–7
public health language 99
Public Health Nurses 96
public health professionals 95
public health programs 92–4

public policy disasters 25
public webpages, development of 97–8
Pushback Network 21

racial inequalities, historic 18
racial inequities, MDRII 89
racial residential segregation 44, 49
racial segregation 45, 49, 80–1
Rawls' argument, component of 34
Rawls' theory of justice 31–2
ReGenesis Economic Development Organization 54
ReGenesis Project 52–4, 53–4
regional accessibility: argument 34; key concepts of justice 31–4; strategies and outcomes 27–31
regional analysis, types of 2
regional anti-poverty strategies 27
regional coalition-building 6
regional collaboration, urban sprawl 75
Regional Contribution Agreements 12, 28
regional equity: field 8, 10; movement 5, 18, 19, 20, 38; proponents 19, 20; strategies 4, 21
regional equity framing (Michigan and Detroit) 79–80; segregation 80; sprawl 79–80
Regional Equity summits 9
regional fair share housing 27
Regional Growth Strategies (RGS) 94, 100
regional Health Authority 98
Regional Housing Needs Assessment 28
regionalism 6–7, 25–7; dispersal, mobility, and alternative conceptions of justice 34–7; regional accessibility strategies and outcomes 27–31
regionalist dispersal programs 38
regional organizing approach 12
regional planning organizations 1
Regional Plan of New York 1929 27
"regional spaces" 10
regional transit authority 7
regulations under Appendix 2. Section 120 105–6
"renewed centrality" 37
request for proposal (RFP), MDRII 82
residential segregation 44, 45, 56
resource pathogens 48
RFP *see* request for proposal
RGS *see* Regional Growth Strategies
"right to the city" 37
Right to the City Alliance 21
riskscapes 47

Safe Drinking Water Act 56
salutogens, in human ecosystems 48–9
Sanitary and Improvement District (SID) 72
sanitation 93

# INDEX

San Jose Chamber of Commerce 13
Santa Clara County Central Labor Council 13
SCOPE 10, 11, 14, 15
"Second National Summit, The" 5
segregation, regional equity framing (Michigan and Detroit) 80
SES *see* socioeconomic status
SID *see* Sanitary and Improvement District
Smart Growth America 9, 63
Smart Growth Network 62–3, 65, 67, 73
Smart Growth principles 73, 74; Davenport, Iowa 69–70; Omaha, Nebraska 72; Springfield, Missouri 67, 68; Wichita, Kansas 70, 71
"smart growth" rules 9
social consciousness by spatial scale, levels of 11, **11**
Social Equity Caucus 13, 15
social goods 33
social movement: approach 10; mobilization 10; regionalism 4, 6, 7, 10–12, 14; regionalists 15, 21–2
social pathogens 48
socioeconomic status (SES) 44
sprawl: categories of 79; regional equity framing (Michigan and Detroit) 79–80
sprawl management 75; analysis of 67; approaches to 74, **74**
Springfield, Missouri: CUMP index 67–8; urban sprawl 67–9; *USA Today*'s sprawl index 67
stakeholders, identification of: health authority staff 95–9; local government staff 99–103; relationships between employees and 96
stakeholders, MDRII planning process 82
state of equity 2
"stealth equity" 9
stressed suburbs, sprawl 79
suburban sprawl 62
Surface Transportation Policy Project 9
system-wide approach: components of 96–8; consultation process with stakeholders 97; HCE initiative 96–7; optimizing communication and consultation activities 97; tool development 97–8
Sze, Julie 45

targeted regional planning 90
Task Force Blueprint report 49
tensions and tightropes 12–13; business 13–15; communities 15–18
territorial government, healthcare programs 93
Title VI of Civil Right Act 55, 56

Tourism Industry Development Corporation 17
Transit Development Plan 70
Transportation Equity Network 21

uneven fiscal development, Michigan 80
urban antipoverty policy 37
Urban Development 27
urban growth policy community 62
urban metropolitan communities 44–5
urban planning, public health and 92–3
urban poor communities 44
urban poverty: policy for 36; remedies for 25
urban renewal projects 36
Urban Service Area Policy 71
urban sprawl 61–2; Davenport, Iowa 69–70; measuring sprawl and effectiveness of growth management 64–5; methodology 65–7; Omaha, Nebraska 71–3; smart growth network 62–3; Springfield, Missouri 67–9; Wichita, Kansas 70–1
urban–suburban disparities 26
US anti-poverty policy 36
*USA Today*'s sprawl index 65–7, 73; Davenport, Iowa 69; Omaha, Nebraska 71; Springfield, Missouri 67; Wichita, Kansas 70
US Department of Housing 27
US Department of Transportation (DOT) 53
US Environmental Protection Agency 71

V8-Gateway *see* Van Dyke/8 Mile Gateway Collaborative
Van Dyke/8 Mile Gateway Collaborative (V8-Gateway) 84–5, 88
Villaraigosa 20

"walkable community" 70
WERA *see* West End Revitalization Association
West End community 54
West End Revitalization Association (WERA) 54–6; communities 55; research on basic amenities 56
white suburban communities 19
Wichita, Kansas: CUMP index 70; urban sprawl 70–1; *USA Today*'s sprawl index 70
Williams, David 44
Wilson, William Julius 44
Wisconsin Regional Training Partnership 16, 18
workforce development system 35
Working Partnerships Leadership Institute 17
Workplace Hollywood 15

Youth Power 84